The Workshop

The Workshop

CELEBRATING
THE PLACE
WHERE
CRAFTSMANSHIP
BEGINS

SCOTT GIBSON

PHOTOGRAPHS BY RANDY O'ROURKE

The Taunton Press

The Taunton Press
Inspiration for hands-on living®

The Taunton Press, Inc., 63 South Main Street, PO Box 5506, Newtown, CT 06470-5506
e-mail: tp@taunton.com

Distributed by Publishers Group West

EDITOR: Stefanie Ramp
JACKET/COVER DESIGN: Susan Fazekas
INTERIOR DESIGN AND LAYOUT: Susan Fazekas
ILLUSTRATOR: Christine Erikson
PHOTOGRAPHER: Randy O'Rourke

Library of Congress Cataloging-in-Publication Data

Gibson, Scott, 1951-
  The workshop : celebrating the place where craftsmanship begins /
Scott Gibson.
     p. cm.
  ISBN 1-56158-575-0
1. Workshops. 2. Woodwork. 3. Woodworkers. I. Title.
TT152 .G53 2003
684'.08–dc21
                              2003004022

Printed in Singapore
10 9 8 7 6 5 4 3 2 1

The following manufacturers/names appearing in *The Workshop* are trademarks: Aeronca™, Altendorf®, Conover®,
Delta®, Disney®, L.L. Bean®, McDonald's®, Shopsmith™, and Woodburst®.

for Susan

Acknowledgments

I am deeply indebted to the furniture makers, turners, carvers, and other artisans whose shops appear in this book. Gracious, honest, open—they were all of these things, no matter what their individual interests and pursuits. Many of them work in solo shops without the kind of help that we may take for granted. There were rarely office assistants to answer the telephone or tend to business while they talked. Yet they willingly stepped away from their work, answered every question, and then endured the follow-up inquiries that came later.

Many of these artisans are commercially successful, some of them at the top of their craft. Their work is shown in private and public collections all over the country. Even so, none has been made wealthy by his or her trade in quite the way our culture has enriched so many other professions. Our world is a vastly more interesting place because they don't seem to mind.

I would also like to thank Stefanie Ramp, my editor, and Helen Albert at The Taunton Press for their help in bringing this project to fruition.

Contents

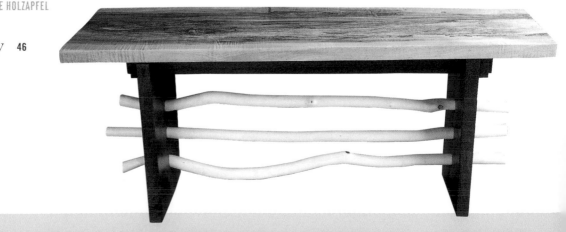

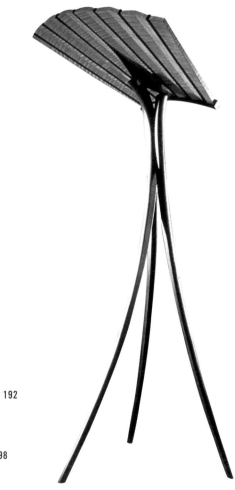

Introduction

THERE IS NO PERFECT WORKSHOP. Any image conjured up by one woodworker would probably be less than ideal for the next. There are, however, many wonderful shops. Contemporary woodworkers share a common cultural heritage with a nation of resourceful settlers who made do with what could be patched together. Hundreds of years later, we still manage to find places to set up our tools and work, no matter where we live. If the basement or garage workshop has become the icon of the weekend do-it-yourselfer, woodworkers have also made themselves comfortably at home in endlessly creative spaces. At its simplest, a shop doesn't take much to be successful: a bit of roof, a bench, and a corner where a tool chest can be stored.

The workshops in this book were chosen because they fairly represent the diverse spaces in which American woodworkers now find themselves. There are shops in recycled button factories, two-car garages, white clapboard buildings in tiny New England villages, old onion barns, industrial parks, and strip malls. Many

woodworkers looking through these pages will think of a favorite shop they've seen—their own or one they've visited—and wonder why it has not been included. No list could possibly be complete, but there is some common ground here. Nearly all of the shops in this book are relatively small, just big enough for one or two woodworkers. Not counting the woodworking schools, the largest covers roughly 9,000 sq. ft. If that seems generous by most standards, it is still nothing more than a speck compared with the factories that produce much of the nation's furniture and woodenware.

Woodworkers prove as diverse as their shops. Some keep their workspaces fastidiously clean. Their tools are carefully arranged in drawers and on walls, and not a single wood shaving litters the floor. At the other end of the spectrum are spaces seemingly arranged by happenstance. Tools, lumber, furniture parts, and bits of hardware lie abandoned where they were last needed. Woodworkers who have been in the same space for many years often accumulate an agreeable clutter that makes them feel at home. Walls are painted or decorated with photographs torn from magazines or postcards. For others, a shop itself seems to hold little inherent interest; it's just four walls and a roof.

However different they may look, all of these shops exude an air of creativity and inventiveness. Each is a place where an artisan, professional or amateur, turns raw materials that could be almost anything into an object that is only one thing. Whether the piece is sold, given away, or ends up in the dining room of the person who made it hardly matters.

What can we learn from a tour of nearly three dozen small woodshops? Something, I hope. Most woodworkers seem curious about the workshops of others. And while these profiles of shops and their owners are not intended as technical descriptions of lighting, wiring, dust collection, or lumber storage, nor as recommendations on what kind of vise or table saw to buy, a detail in a photograph or a woodworker's description of his work habits may suggest a solution to another woodworker who has been wrestling with the same problem. In truth, however, most of these details are no more important than the intent and expectations we bring to our work—maybe less. Great shops are really a combination of all of these things, not only how we arrange the space and stock it with tools and raw materials but also how we use the space when we get there.

Shops are more than places where work gets done. They're personal spaces, too.

The Workshop Legacy

MY FATHER'S chairmaking shop was once a shed on the back of my parents' house in upstate New York. It was separated from the house and given a new identity when they made room for a new addition.

MY FATHER WORKED FOR YEARS in a tiny workshop behind his house in upstate New York. The workshop had originally been a shed attached to the back of the house, but the shed was in the way when my parents went ahead with plans for an addition. Rather than demolish this little building, they asked the builder to drag it out of the way. He moved it 100 ft. and set it on a foundation of concrete blocks. There was barely enough room inside for a bandsaw, a lathe, and a 5-ft. bench.

INSIDE, THERE WAS barely room for a small bench, a lathe, and a bandsaw, yet my father worked in his workshop for nearly 20 years without complaint, turning out scores of Windsor chairs and assorted pieces of furniture.

SMALL PROFESSIONAL shops are places of employment where people can earn their daily bread. Although shops are often festooned with favorite memorabilia, they also can be stark, even cold. The carver who works here likes a plain space because it does not intrude on his work.

As small as it was, the shop was serviceable, and it appealed to my father's sense of economy. There was so little storage that he stockpiled planks of lumber in a barn a few miles away. When he needed a board he would drive over, tie the lumber to the roof of his car, and drive home.

My father made Windsor chairs: continuous and sack-back armchairs, writing-arms, bowbacks, and benches. He had enough room to make one chair at a time, which is what he preferred doing, so the shop fulfilled its most important role. And the longer he worked there, the more at home he seemed. It was jammed with fixtures and jigs for chairmaking, racks of drill bits and hand tools, boxes of sandpaper and spring clamps, ankle-deep shavings around the lathe, and lengths of wood leaning against the walls. And it was all *his* stuff. He was at liberty to smoke a cigar and listen to Fats Waller without drawing complaints on either count.

Twenty-five years after the workshop was moved, my parents sold the house. I helped my father wrap his tools in newspaper and pack them into cardboard boxes. When the building was nearly empty, I realized the life had gone out of it. By itself, it really didn't have any magic. What had given the shop its charm was the familiarity of everything in it: the tools, the conversations, the half-assembled chairs, and the smell of the place on a wet afternoon. It was, in the end, just a small, shingled shed.

A few years later, I packed up my own shop in preparation for a move and had exactly the same experience. We had erected the building nine years earlier; it was one large room with a high ceiling and a wood-plank floor. I had spent a lot of time there. I made furniture, but like all good workshops, it also became a general workroom. We fixed garden tools, made cabinets for the house, repaired old chairs and tables, and worked on chainsaws and seized-up string trimmers.

I had the place to myself for a few years, but as my son grew older, he began to wander out and look for things to do. I then had to worry not only about *my* fingers on the table saw but his as well. The point of it, I remember thinking as I packed up my stuff, was that the workshop had seeped into the family's collective experience. It was as familiar as any room in our house. When the room was empty, I thought of my dad's old shop; what I was leaving was just a big room.

I set up a new shop in a two-car garage behind the house we'd just bought. It was a train wreck of a place. It needed heat, new wiring, insulation, and a new roof. When I reframed the front wall, I found a mammoth nest of carpenter ants in the soggy carrying timber that was holding up the second floor. But the shop is on the mend. It's more room than I've ever had, and it has a loft for wood storage. It's also beginning to feel like home. Shops, it turns out, are movable experiences.

What makes it feel like home is having a place for my stuff—the tools I've collected, the lumber, and the odds and ends. Shops are more than places where work gets done; they're personal spaces, too. They're repositories not only for an accumulation of tools, lumber, and hardware but also for a hundred other items that we wouldn't consider keeping in the house.

It makes me think that part of the point of having a shop is to become the curator of your own museum. Shops are never truly finished; they evolve right along with you, changing—and sometimes even moving—to keep up.

The Small-Shop Tradition

Nearly all of the woodworking shops in this book are maintained by professionals. Many of these professionals are furniture makers, but there are also carvers, a luthier, woodworking

GATHERING OLD TOOLS and odds and ends is a time-honored tradition among most woodworkers I've met. My own collection includes things that have no practical value as well as a fine set of old chisels.

DESPITE DIFFERENCES in tools and materials, revolutionary-era cabinetmakers worked in ways similar to contemporary furniture makers with small shops. Furniture is still assembled by hand, and pieces are often made singly or in small batch runs. (Earlier woodworkers, however, had more Cuban mahogany than we do.)

teachers, someone who makes outdoor structures for children, and turners. As owners of small businesses, these craftsmen have a lot in common with the original tradesmen who worked in a Colonial Williamsburg cabinetmaking shop more than 250 years ago (see the photo at bottom left). In some ways, the craft hasn't changed much since then.

Contemporary craftsmen have a wider selection of materials and better tools, but the process of making something from wood is essentially the same. Furniture is drawn on paper (well, maybe using a computer), then each component is cut and shaped by a single craftsman. He or she assembles and finishes the piece and delivers it to the person who ordered it. Art furniture or sculptural pieces may evolve differently, but an essential similarity is the methodology of work: a deliberate one-at-a-time approach. Customers may wait for months—years even—before their orders are filled. They could just as easily drive to a local retail store and buy what they wanted the same day—and for less money. That so many professional artisans are able to make a living is an encouraging sign that there are still people who assign a high value to this approach and are willing to pay for it.

Even the busiest production shops in this book—Green Design Furniture in Portland, Maine (see p. 80), or the Nakashima Studios in Pennsylvania (see p. 86)—move at a snail's pace compared to the furniture industry as a whole. Furniture making in a small shop, is a completely different process. A craftsman makes dozens of decisions—how to match the figure in adjoining pieces of wood, how wide to make a table apron, whether a leg should be turned or cut square—about each piece he or she makes. No one suggests that the process is as economical or efficient as that found in a furniture factory, but then again it's not supposed to be.

In his book *The Nature and Art of Workmanship*, David Pye, an English craftsman and intellectual, offers what is probably the most widely repeated explanation of what distinguishes craft from mass production. He explains two ways of working. One is a process whose outcome is predetermined, which he calls the "workmanship of certainty." That is, the worker uses machines or techniques that eliminate the risk of an unplanned outcome. With the other approach, the "workmanship of risk," there are no guaranteed outcomes. Pye describes this kind of craftsmanship as "using any kind of technique or apparatus in which the quality of the result is not predetermined, but depends on the judgment, dexterity and care which the maker exercises as he works. The essential idea is that the quality of the result is continually at risk during the process of making."

The line between these two approaches is fuzzy, not solid, and both are usually found in the same small shop. For example, Christian Becksvoort (see p. 104) uses a horizontal boring machine to cut mortises in the cherry Shaker-style furniture he makes. This is what Pye would call the "workmanship of certainty." Yet Becksvoort cuts by hand all joints that show in a finished piece. He forms dovetails with a handsaw and chops them out with a chisel and a mallet. If he starts thinking about what's for dinner and the tool slips, he ruins the joint.

SOME FURNITURE MAKERS have turned to computers for creating shop drawings and for revising designs, but many more still set pencil to paper. Drawings give makers the chance to work out joinery and proportion in advance: Erasers are cheaper than cherry.

FACTORIES THEY'RE NOT

Even with the best tools, few artisans in small shops have the efficiencies of a factory. There are exceptions, but it is fundamentally a different process in intent as well as practice. A few years ago, I toured a kitchen-cabinet factory in the Midwest. This gigantic operation had a million square feet under roof. Hundreds of people worked there. Many of them stood on production lines all day, where they would perform the same task over and over again without seeing the finished product.

Cabinets were assembled from component parts that could be made in advance and then stockpiled. When a customer ordered a particular cabinet configuration and color, the parts were pulled from waiting inventories and routed to a team of assemblers. Within a few minutes, workers were able to glue and nail the cabinets together, hang the doors, and box up the cabinets for shipping. As far as industry standards go, these cabinets were fairly good quality. But no one would confuse them with studio furniture.

All of us buy mass-produced goods, whether that means kitchen cabinets, turned woodenware, or automobiles. No one could afford to buy only handmade work. But when we do, the relationship between buyer and producer suddenly becomes important. What the artisan, and presumably the customer, wants is the maximum possible interaction with raw materials and design. Even if the maker manages the shop efficiently, the work will cost more than a piece made in a factory. Customers know they are getting something different, and they're willing to pay more for it. That's the deal.

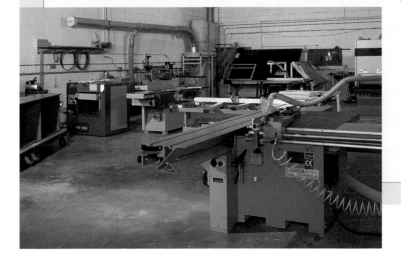

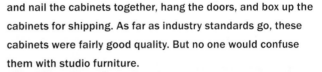

WHILE MANY small shops are still using conventional power and hand tools, some furniture makers are taking advantage of factorylike machines that follow computerized instructions. Production is both faster and more accurate and in a small shop, they allow the artisan to retain a personal relationship with his customers.

VIRTUALLY ALL profes-
sional furniture makers
use stationary power
tools for stock prepara-
tion, shaping, and even
joinery. Yet most period
furniture demands hand-
cut joinery when it shows
in a finished piece. Suc-
cessfully blending hand
and machine techniques
often becomes a small
shop's market niche.

SMALL SHOPS, even tiny shops, can be as
enriching for amateurs as large spaces. Professionals earning a living on what they produce usually need more room than what this
shop affords, but a great deal of fine work
can be made in very tight quarters.

That is the essential difference between furniture that is made in a factory and furniture made in a small shop. Even though most amateur
woodworkers use machines to speed up the work and make the outcome more predictable, few completely eliminate the element of risk
in how a piece will turn out. In this, amateur woodworkers the world
over are allied with small-shop professionals.

The Commonality of a Tradition

Most of the artisans in this book have a basic repertoire of tools that
will look familiar to any part-time woodworker. At the heart of most
shops, you can find a heavy-duty table saw or bandsaw, a thickness
planer, and a jointer. Almost everyone needs these items. In addition,
there may be a collection of more specialized tools that are related to a
particular trade—a scrollsaw for someone who cuts intricate patterns or
a heavy mortising machine for someone who does a lot of casework.
With some exceptions, they are often the same kinds of tools that can
be found in many amateur shops.

Their tools, however, are rarely cheap. Many a bad piece of furniture is unfairly blamed on the tools used to make it, but it is also true
that first-rate work is infinitely more difficult with poorly made tools.

A number of these woodworkers like old tools—big
cast-iron models made 50 years or 60 years ago. Some are
even older. William Turner, Michael Fortune, Kevin
Rodel, Scott Schmidt, and a number of others all own one
or more stationary power tools that have been salvaged
from previous work sites, reconditioned, and put back into
service. Many are far more handsome than their modern
equivalents, with graceful, curved castings and delicate or-
namentation that manufacturers no longer bother with. In
other shops, technology has been harnessed in imaginative
ways. Vacuum-actuated clamps and veneer presses, high-
pressure water nozzles, and computer-guided overhead
routers have all vastly increased accuracy and productivity.

Many shops are also stocked with a good selection of
hand tools. Even in shops where machines do a lot of the
work, it is not at all unusual to see a wall-mounted tool
chest that neatly stores handplanes, chisels, cabinet scrapers, files, marking gauges, and a dozen other tools. Some
of the shops rely almost completely on hand tools, but

A COLLECTION of hand tools burnished with years of hard use is a focal point in the shops of many professionals, even as power equipment becomes more sophisticated and more affordable.

most of these furniture makers seem to have reached a compromise: using machines to eliminate drudgery and using hand tools when they are faster.

Preserving the Workshop Tradition

Keeping the workshop tradition alive is an uphill fight. One of the furniture makers I visited, someone doing really first-rate work, told me he earns about $40,000 a year. We are becoming a culture that doesn't know how to make a living with our hands. Indeed, the federal labor department reports the fastest-growing occupations in the next decade will be computer engineers, computer-support specialists, system analysts, database administrators, desktop publishers, paralegals, and home health aides. Nowhere on the top 10 list will you find anything connected with a manual trade. This will make small amateur workshops all the more important. They will remain places where even analysts, database administrators, and paralegals can experience what Pye calls the "workmanship of risk."

PRESERVING THE WORKSHOP TRADITION

Along with everyone else in the seventh grade at the Robert E. Bell School, I was required to take a shop class. It lasted half a year. I can't remember the name of our teacher, but he had a short brush cut and wore a short-sleeve white shirt and metal-rim glasses. We had our choice of projects. I made a hammered-copper ashtray and a turned bowl from walnut and maple. Back in those days, seventh graders were allowed to use power tools. Most schools are different now. Some shop teachers have modified tools that can be run without electricity (see p.68), and many other programs have been abandoned altogether.

The type of experience I had with shop class has been supplanted by something educators call "technology education." Rather than make a birdhouse or magazine rack, students are more likely to study hydraulics, robotics, agriscience, or solar-powered cars. Schools want higher test scores for their students, not more copper ashtrays. Although there are exceptions, old-line shop teachers are "graying out and being pushed out," as one educator puts it. The intent may be admirable as technology threatens to engulf us, but how many seventh graders will make solar-powered cars and robots in their garages and basements when they are middle aged?

WHAT HAPPENED to shop class? Once standard fare, old-fashioned industrial arts classes are dying out. Left unchecked, the trend may saddle us with a thousand white-collar professionals for each craftsman who can make a serviceable chair.

"Since I write for do-it-yourself, weekend carpenters, I purposely limit myself to using only the most essential tools in my shop."

Backyard Simplicity

DAVID STILES—who, with his wife, writes how-to books on building and carpentry—built a simple backyard workshop. A skylight helps keep power bills low by providing ample natural light.

THE SMALL STRUCTURE behind David Stiles's East Hampton, New York, home is a quintessential backyard shop. Simple in both design and construction, the building measures only 10 ft. by 14 ft. It is, he says, the minimum size he needs to accommodate his tools while still giving him enough room to move around. But it's just enough. Inside, a radial-arm saw and small table saw are lined up on one wall and, on the other, a narrow bench with shelves and drawers for storing tools and hardware. Stiles framed the building with 4x6 cedar, covered it with

panels of insulation, and sheathed the building with a type of exterior plywood called T1-11. With a plywood floor and only a portable electric heater to ward off the chill, the shop is reminiscent of an old-fashioned woodshed where a favorite uncle might be found puttering on a rainy Saturday morning.

Nothing Extraneous

Both the scale of the building and its contents have been carefully planned. Stiles and his wife, Jean Trusty Stiles, write how-to books: 15 of them, so far, on everything from building gazebos and sheds to carpentry for beginners. During the week, the couple works in New York City. Their home and shop near the eastern end of Long Island are mainly for weekend and summer use, and Stiles tailored it to fit both professional and personal needs. "Since I write for do-it-yourself, weekend carpenters, I purposely limit myself to using only the most essential tools in my shop," he says.

He keeps only basic power tools: a small table saw, a radial-arm saw, a benchtop drill press, and a small electric grinder. There are the inevitable jars of screws and nails, the cans of paint, and the clamps hung over the workbench—in all, the tools and equipment that would be available to most any homeowner who had a small corner of the yard to spare for a workshop and a limited budget with which to stock it. Stiles chose not to make room for a jointer, thickness planer, shaper, or bandsaw. Giving up the heavy, stationary power tools that are the mainstay of most professional cabinet or furniture shops keeps Stiles tuned to the needs of his audience. If he can design and build a project in his own small workshop, using a limited number of power tools, he hopes that his readers may be encouraged to do the same.

The same reasoning went into sizing the building. His East Hampton lot would have been able to accommodate a slightly larger building but the home woodworkers Stiles needs to connect with are unlikely to own big dream shops with unlimited space for tools, lumber, and works in progress.

Making the Most of It

Because his shop is peanut size, Stiles included some practical detailing designed to make the most of the space he has. He built a skylight into the roof and triangular windows in the peaks of both gable-end walls to provide more natural light. They also help cut electric bills.

Doors can be opened at both ends of the shop so that he can rip a board of any length on the table saw without running it into a wall. The table for his radial-arm saw is the same height as the bed of the table saw to support lumber as it is being ripped.

Try as he might to keep the building compact but efficient, Stiles did run out of room for lumber as his shop began to fill with tools. His solution was a 30-in. extension of the roof on one side of the building to create a small "lumber library," as he calls it. Neatly stacked on shelves inside are the boards, panel goods, and offcuts that otherwise would take up valuable floor space inside the shop. The

A 14-FT. BY 10-FT. SHOP may not be palatial, but it is enough for the basics. Stiles limited tools to those that most weekend woodworkers were likely to own, making a big shop unnecessary.

BY OPENING DOORS at both ends of the shop, Stiles can rip long boards without fear of banging into walls or tools.

BENCH TEST

A licensed house builder, David Stiles still enjoys putting up small structures. His projects have included a seaside summerhouse (shown in the photo at right), whose exterior brackets and finial were made in his backyard workshop. Built a few years ago for clients whose house overlooks Three Mile Harbor on Long Island, the 12-ft.-wide octagonal structure has combination doors whose glass panels can be replaced by screens in the summer.

For some friends with a Tudor-style house, Stiles built an 8-ft. by 12-ft. storage building to match (shown in the photo below) and included his own shopmade window frames made of cedar. Stiles enjoys keeping his hand in as a builder, even if the scale is small, and the projects give him a chance to test ideas that will later appear in book form.

BOTH AUTHOR
AND BUILDER,
David Stiles
made component
parts for these
two buidlings in
his backyard
shop, a structure
measuring only
140 sq. ft.

addition also satisfied Stiles's design sense. It transformed a plain, gable-roof shed into a more interesting saltbox shape.

Jack of All Trades

To verify dimensions and forestall potential construction problems, Stiles often builds the projects he writes about, so his shop is a kind of test bed for many of the projects he later describes in book form. But not everything can be built in so small a space. When the project is a structure that will be assembled on-site, Stiles can still make some of the components—cabinets, windows, trim—in his workshop and move them to the job site when they're needed.

Stiles has found a way to blend many interests. A designer and illustrator as well as a licensed builder, he has worked for a number of New York architectural firms. With his wife, he has written a stack of books as well as articles for a long list of magazines. And, yet, a tiny, decidedly low-tech workshop is where his heart still lies. "I love my shop," he says. "It gives me great pleasure to be able to build things that help my family and myself live better."

RUNNING OUT of room inside the shop for lumber storage, Stiles extended the roof on one side of the building to provide covered storage. A wooden latch prevents the door from closing in the wind.

A SAVVY DOORSTOP

Winds blowing off Long Island Sound can raise havoc with the door on David Stiles's shop. His solution was to create a notched wooden arm that pivots upward to capture the top edge of the door and hold it next to the wall of the shop. When he wants to disengage the door, Stiles tugs on a rope that loops through a screw eye and down to the arm.

Door Latch

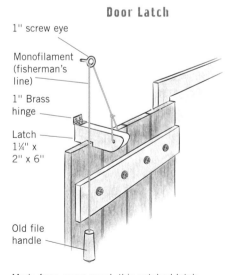

1" screw eye

Monofilament (fisherman's line)

1" Brass hinge

Latch 1¼" x 2" x 6"

Old file handle

Made from scrap wood, this notched latch is mounted to the wall behind the door and securely holds it open until the string is pulled.

Where a traditional
furniture maker would
use a straight piece
of wood, Brooks uses
a tree limb in all its
irregular glory.

Nature in the Rough

A SCULPTURE OF WOOD
frames the workshop of Jon
Brooks, a New Hampshire
artist and furniture maker
who rebelled at the idea of
living or working in a boxy
structure of straight lines and
predictable proportions. The
small, second-story bumpout
is Brooks's office.

J ON BROOKS DREAMED all through high school of
moving west and living in California, and for a
while, it looked as though he might make it. He
got as far as looking at land in Mendocino on California's
northern coast in the early 1970s.

But a variety of circumstances brought him back to
New Hampshire, and now, some 30 years later, he views
it as the center of the universe. "Not the center of *my* universe," he says, deadpan, "the center of *the* universe."
There are gallery and business contacts, friends, his own

LIKE HIS HOUSE several hundred feet up the hill, the workshop has a contoured-roof form. Behind the shop is a building used by apprentices that seek Brooks out and stay for as long as two years.

AN ELM LOG shaped with a chainsaw became a ladder to a tiny second-floor office over the shop floor. Brooks cut the log green and then sealed it with several coats of diluted white glue. Thirty years later, it shows no signs of checking or cracking.

sculptures planted in the fields around him, and a house and shop that so closely reflect his interests and artistic outlook that it's difficult to imagine Brooks living anywhere else.

No Square Corners

Brooks never imagined himself living in a box, and the house he built off a dirt road in rural New Hampshire will never be confused with a raised ranch. "Artkamp," as he calls it, is a mix of materials and shapes. With its contoured roof, exposed framing, and stair stringers hewn from whole trees, the house is unpretentious and warm but also an intensely individual artistic expression. The house also is a good introduction to Brooks's workshop a short walk down the hill. It, too, is a long way from being conventional.

Only 18 ft. on a side, the shop in plan is a rhombus—a geometric shape that looks like a squashed square with walls of equal length but no right angles. Its contoured, swaybacked roof rises to meet a tiny second-story bumpout where Brooks has an office (access is from inside the shop via a chainsaw-carved ladder made from an elm log). Over the back door is a triangular roof overhang that looks as though it might be a hinged table leaf.

Around back, on the side of the building facing the road, the second-floor office now appears suspended over a small porch. Tall windows take up most of one wall as they rise to a peaked gable. Shingles covering the building (some of them split by hand) are arranged in irregular rows that manage to make the building look as if it's stretching in its skin.

Brooks built the shop on a shoestring. He had a homesteader's sensibilities when he started, believing that if he could find a

A RHOMBUS IN PLAN, Brooks's shop measures 18 ft. on a side. Although he owns an industrial bandsaw, a lathe, and other power tools, the nature of Brooks's craft calls for careful work done by hand, not by machine. A single chair may be two months in the making.

START WITH STICKS

The work of Jon Brooks blurs the line between sculpture and furniture. Making the most of natural materials available in the wooded hills around his New Hampshire home, Brooks combines the unpredictable, organic shapes of saplings with highly figured sawn lumber.

Although Brooks may start with a sketch, he often allows designs to be shaped by the materials he gathers. Pieces are frequently decorated with carved hieroglyphs and colored pencils, then protected with a clear top coat. Brooks has exhibited his work in both the United States and Europe, and his furniture is in a number of collections, including the American Craft Museum and the Renwick Gallery.

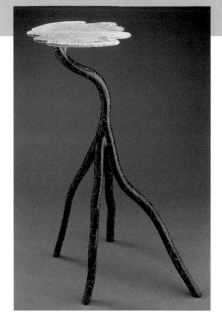

"EVERGLADES CLOUD TABLE": Maple saplings support a polished top of curly maple to form a table inspired by a trip to the Florida Everglades.

"CURLY STYX LADDERBAX": A matching pair of ladderback armchairs in maple, 78 in. high, uses sugar maple saplings for legs, back rails, and rungs. Seats, arms, and back slats are curly maple.

"ONE VOICE": This piece provides back-to-back seating on a base representing a howling coyote. Maple tree limbs up to 3 in. in diameter form the base. Seats and backs are figured maple finished in oil and varnish.

suitable piece of land the rest would naturally follow. With thrift and self-sufficiency in mind, he built the shop on concrete piers—not only fast and inexpensive but decidedly low-tech. After 30 years in the same space, he's starting to plan an addition.

Taking Nature's Lead

Branches of maple and ash are Brooks's favored building materials, and he can gather them locally. Wood is stripped of its bark, marked as to species and the date it was cut, and stored in a shed behind his shop until he's ready to use it. To a furniture maker dealing in conventional forms, his stockpiled raw materials would look something like a shed full of kindling and stove wood.

But to Brooks, the crooked branches and tree parts are a perfect starting point. He makes both functional and nonfunctional pieces, and it would be hard to describe his furniture to anyone who hasn't seen it. Start with rustic furniture—pieces made from found material like tree branches—and add color, finish, and sculptural shapes. Where a traditional furniture-maker would use a straight piece of wood, Brooks uses a tree limb in all its irregular glory. There are, in fact, few straight lines to be found in his work. Surfaces may be dyed, decorated with colored pencils, and then lacquered, so that sculpted wood takes on the look of an entirely different material.

Little Tooling Around

Brooks makes some of the parts he needs from standard sawn lumber. But because natural shapes are so central to his work, he makes do with few of the stationary power tools that straight-line cabinetmakers need. He has a combination thickness planer-jointer tucked against a wall and a relatively small lathe. Hanging from a length of wire

STRIPPED OF ITS BARK, a maple pole will be marked with a date and stored in a shed behind the shop. Brooks uses sawn lumber sparingly, more often making major furniture components from found wood whose crooks and twists take on a sculptural look.

BROOKS TRIMS BRANCHES gathered in the woods near his home—one essential ingredient for his sculptural furniture. His sawhorses were made by an apprentice who announced one day that Brooks needed a new pair. "Go for it," Brooks told him.

near the backdoor is a small, electric chainsaw. A variety of hand tools hang from the walls.

While there is no table saw, no shaper, and no compound miter saw, there is a giant bandsaw, which dominates one side of the shop. It came from a box factory in Fitzwilliam, New Hampshire. Originally driven by a belt, the bandsaw takes a blade 18 ft. 6 in. long and has babbitt bearings that Brooks rebored when he bought the machine. He has no idea how old the bandsaw is.

Brooks may not need an extensive collection of power tools, but he does rely on several carving vises to hold irregularly shaped pieces of wood. Mounted to a bench or other surface with a single threaded bolt and hand-tightened nut, the vises can be moved quickly and used in tandem to accommodate extralong pieces of wood.

Room for Two

His shop would seem small for many solo furniture makers, yet Brooks has had a regular stream of apprentices for more than 30 years. They stay between six months and more than two years, working on their own projects or helping Brooks with his. Brooks doesn't go looking for them. They find him, and some of them simply show up at the door. Until 10 years ago, apprentices often stayed in a small building right next to the shop. Now, he is more likely to take on someone who lives in the area, so they can live at home and commute to work.

Apprentices typically have a woodworking background or have recently come through a fine arts program. They're looking for experience in a working studio in advance of setting up their own, and Brooks likes the interaction. He recalls one apprentice, a recent graduate of the Rhode Island School of Design, who brought with him some practical innovations for the shop. "It was great," he says. "He said, 'Jon, why are you doing it this way when you could do this?'

"SPIRAL PILLARS," a series of wood sculptures by Brooks, stretch along the walkway between Brooks's house and his workshop. To Brooks, they suggest what might be left after a major structure, such as a cathedral, gradually went to ruin.

That sort of thing is really wonderful." As important as the feedback Brooks gets on his work is an exchange of aesthetics that wouldn't happen if Brooks were to work by himself.

Exchanging ideas with fellow artists can be helpful, but Brooks doesn't stop there. He's just as likely to ask people who know nothing about art for comments on his current work. "I love feedback," he says. He talks with a local woodcutter, the guy who delivers propane, and the UPS driver. If he senses some engagement, he's likely to ask for an opinion—not so much what they think of his work in general but what they might do specifically to a piece he's currently working on. They may not change his mind, but he's interested just the same. Who knows what can happen?

Cooper's "core product" is not so much furniture or carving but the reaction it evokes in people who use it, especially children.

Carving Delight

COOPER'S TWO-ROOM SHOP covers a total of 1,600 sq. ft. Its main room is big enough for both Cooper and a woodworking roommate, while an adjacent area has been turned into storage and office space.

IKE THE BUTTON FACTORY a few blocks away (see Scott Schmidt's shop on p. 182), the low brick building where Jeffrey Cooper keeps his shop was not originally intended as a space for woodworking. Constructed as a shoe shop in the 1930s, the building looks like a place where crates of textbooks or surplus machine parts might be stored.

Windows on the first and second floors are sealed with concrete block and metal shutters. Third-floor windows are mostly opaque glass block, suggesting that

A HIPPO TAKES SHAPE under Cooper's drawing pencil, representative of his art furniture with animal themes. Blocks of wood are stack-laminated before they are shaped.

A DEPRESSION-ERA shoe factory in Portsmouth, New Hampshire, has been chopped into a warren of locked storage rooms on the first two floors. But the top floor houses a variety of artisans, making a creative community that includes furniture maker and carver Jeffrey Cooper.

if anyone did work up there they wouldn't be interested in the view. Two-thirds of the building, in fact, is a kind of warehouse. Behind padlocked metal doors on the first two floors are storage lockers rented out by the building's owner. Only when visitors ascend to the third floor will they find much human activity, and suddenly there is a lot of it: a dance studio, a furniture refinisher, antique restorers, a sculptor, a painter, and a computer-software salesperson.

Finding Community

Down near the end of the hall is Cooper's 1,600-sq.-ft. space, an area he shares with another woodworker. "My building has a community," Cooper says. "Having my own place by a house in the countryside sounds romantic and all, but I like my building."

Cooper's shop is a long, narrow room with a worn wood floor and a high ceiling capped with whitewashed rafters. Next door is a 450-sq.-ft. room that serves as an office and storage space. He has built a collection of solid woodworking equipment typical for most cabinetmakers—a table saw, a bandsaw, a restored 12-in. American jointer, a 12-in. Parks thickness planer—but Cooper's chief interest has become carving.

He builds art furniture with animal themes: a low bench carved and painted to look like a tiger, a floor lamp on which two carved parrots perch, a bed where a horse and rider gallop across the headboard and footboard. While his shop roommate, Michael, works on a classically styled mahogany chest, Cooper is busy carving aquatic dinosaurs on maple panels that will be worked into a staircase balustrade.

His workbenches aren't fancy, but Cooper has three of them of different heights so he can keep the work at a comfortable level no matter what its size. The high bench is for relief carving on wood panels that lie flat. Lower benches are designed for sculpture of different sizes, with the lowest bench doubling as an outfeed table for his jointer when he mills extralong stock.

Changing Directions

Cooper's career as a woodworker started while he was taking courses at the University of New Hampshire. Even as an adult-ed student, Cooper had unrestricted access to the university's woodshop, and he took advantage of it. When he thought he was ready, he bought some tools and went out on his own. He says now that he probably should have stayed in school longer because he was forced to teach himself many of the basic manual skills and marketing skills he would need as a full-time professional. Although the learning curve was long, Cooper thinks one advantage to striking out early is that he did not become too much of a disciple of any one instructor. When he did find his niche, it was unique.

A few years ago, however, Cooper thought his career had stalled. He signed up for a marketing course. He soon realized that what he calls his "core product" is not so much furniture or carving but the reaction it evokes in people who use it, especially children. He didn't have to change his work; he just needed to change the way he was presenting his work to potential customers.

The result was a new company brochure titled "Joy and Delight," the two commodities Cooper says are at the heart of his work as a carver. A new ad showed his young daughter sitting on a chair he had carved in the shape of an animal, and it helped him win a commission from the Texas Children's Hospital. Since then, he's been in touch with parents who say his furniture has provided a lift for their children as they struggled with illness. "When Bailey stayed at Texas Children's Hospital," one woman wrote, "the times he smiled was with your wonderful animal chairs. They really helped him through." The responses have helped Cooper confirm that choosing natural themes for his work was the right decision. "People can get furniture at a furniture store," he says, "but my furniture gives them enjoyment each time they use it."

A BED FRAME combines Cooper's love of carving with more conventional furniture making. He says the nature of his designs makes them inherently fun to make.

What matters most about Michael Creed's studio, like his furniture and sculpture, is not necessarily what you can see from the outside but what lurks beneath the surface.

Furniture as Art

MORE THAN THE USUAL collection of woodworking tools adorns the walls of Michael Creed's studio. Photographs and sketches hint at a feverish imagination that has blossomed into articulated furniture that moves in unexpected ways, along with sculptural treatments of ordinary objects.

ONE LOOK AT THE WORK of Michael Creed would convince anyone that his path to furniture making was something other than conventional. Creed's furniture doesn't just sit there; it usually does something. What looks like a multicolored box on legs, for example, becomes a cat-shaped desk when its tail is cranked. A chair whose back and legs are carved snakes hisses when the sitter stands up. When Creed says he found ordinary jobs ho-hum at best, there is no reason to doubt him.

Two stints with restoration carpenters gave Creed his start. There was no shortage of grand old houses in central Virginia that had fallen into disrepair, and Creed learned that nursing them back to health required both inventiveness and creativity. When Creed decided to move on, he took the basic construction skills he had picked up and added a liberal dollop of his own imagination. The result is functional art, objects that are as much sculpture as they are furniture.

Furniture with Personality

Creed's very first furniture projects were traditional. Then a customer approached him asking for something a little different. Creed responded with the cat desk, "Kattmose II," what he calls his "seminal piece" of art furniture. The response amazed him. The desk helped him get into a craft guild, and it was published in a design textbook, several newspapers, and even an Italian magazine. There was no reason to limit himself to conventional designs.

Creed uses a variety of materials—leather, glass, and steel, as well as wood—for projects that sometimes take more than a year to complete. He usually has more than one piece of furniture underway at a time, preferring to pick away at a project rather than work on one piece start to finish.

Pieces of furniture often include a variety of moving parts, which are not at all apparent on first glance: unexpected doors and drawers, for example, or storage compartments that emerge from a flat surface. The complicated designs delight customers and complement Creed's lifelong fascination with gadgets.

A Shop of Bits and Pieces

What matters most about Michael Creed's studio, like his furniture and sculpture, is not necessarily what you can see from the outside but what lurks beneath the surface. He assembled the original 14-ft. by 32-ft. structure from found as well as purchased material, with the idea that it might someday be moved to a new location. When he and his wife decided to stay where they were, Creed doubled its size. With a thick wisteria

CREED MADE "GRRRROVER" as a sculptural funeral urn for two pets. When the drawer is opened, it releases the hinged top and reveals an upper compartment. It is made from cherry, walnut, and bird's-eye maple.

vine climbing above the entrance and weathered cedar shingles beginning to slide from the roof, the building now looks as if it were planted in the Virginia soil long ago.

Two arched windows that poke up through the roofline to form dormers came from a Gothic church 30 miles south of Lynchburg—"a picture postcard" kind of place. Creed built the shop's roof system from pieces of a ruined tobacco factory in town. The maple floor, laid in a herringbone pattern, came from an old staircase that had been scrapped.

Half of the L-shaped building houses Creed's extensive lumber collection as well as completed pieces of furniture. It is the main workroom that reveals his personality. In addition to the usual collection of woodworking equipment, there is ample evidence of Creed's hard-working imagination. Walls are plastered with photographs, drawings, and shapes cut out of cardboard—all of it there to help Creed decide where his next project will take him.

LOOKING EVERY BIT like a holdover from the last century, Michael Creed's studio in a middle-class neighborhood of Lynchburg, Virginia, was built 20 years ago on giant timber skids so it could be moved. Travel plans were abandoned when Creed's wife finished graduate school and found work locally.

It takes Vesery as long to make a 4-in.-tall teacup as it would most furniture makers to turn out a dining-room table, and he frequently needs just as many tools.

A World of Tiny Details

WITH HARDLY a square inch of room wasted, Vesery finds a shop 20 ft. by 22 ft. to be an ample size for turning and carving. His workbenches are sections of an old bowling alley he found locally and cut to size. Hanging from a jury-rigged stand on his bench are the reciprocating and rotary carving tools vital to his work.

JACQUES VESERY HAS at least one advantage over most of his woodworking friends who make big pieces of furniture: He doesn't need much room. Vesery's turned and intricately carved vessels are rarely more than a foot tall, and most are considerably smaller than that. It takes Vesery as long to make a 4-in.-tall teacup as it would most furniture makers to turn out a dining-room table, and he frequently needs just as many tools. Yet all of his equipment fits neatly in the 20-ft. by 22-ft. garage attached to his house.

At Home in the Garage

It is, by Vesery's count, the fourth garage workshop he's had since he first started tinkering with a lathe some 15 years ago. He was working at the time as a forest ranger in New Jersey and had set up a woodworking-maintenance shop at the camp where he lived. A friend gave him a 1928 Oliver direct-drive lathe that had been in storage for decades. It didn't work, but Vesery dragged it to his workshop and began to untangle its ancient wiring.

Within an hour he had it running, and he began to turn bowls again for the first time since high school. A few years later, he and his wife moved to Maine where she was to begin her medical residency. Vesery decided to stick with woodworking and carpentry, so he took over the two-car garage at the house they rented and turned it into a workshop.

With the blessing of its owner, Vesery installed new windows and insulation and finished the interior walls. He relied on a woodstove for heat. On cold days, he'd have to build a fire by four o'clock in the morning if he hoped to get any work done that day.

What followed was a succession of garage workshops at rented houses until Vesery and his wife bought their own house in Damariscotta, farther east along the coast. "Same thing: two-car garage, temporary shop. And every single time I had to insulate the garage, wallboard the place, and do this," he explained, gesturing around him to his neatly finished work space. On a shelf is a cardboard model he made of the new shop he's thinking about, a 20-ft. by 30-ft. structure he wonders if he'll ever build.

Turn First, Carve Later

Vesery's work begins with a vaselike blank, usually cherry, which he turns—while the wood is still green—on one of several lathes he owns

LEAVES AND FEATHERS are a recurring theme in the work of Maine turner and carver Jacques Vesery. Completed in 2000, "Washing the Shadows from My Pillow" (above) is a 4-in.-high vase in dyed cherry with a rim of amboyna burl and an interior of 23-karat gold leaf.

LEAVES AND FEATHERS are roughly outlined and carved with handheld power tools, and Vesery brings a number of pieces to this point before adding fine details with burning tools. This final step in the process consumes days, even weeks—what his wife estimates only as "countless hours."

(at one time he had seven). He may turn a dozen hollow vessels a day, cycling them in short bursts through a microwave oven tucked beneath his bench until they are thoroughly dried.

Although it's easy to think of Vesery as a turner, he completes most of his turning in about two weeks a year. What follows is the transformation of the smooth outer surface of a blank into a detailed layer of feathers or leaves, a process that takes days and sometimes weeks. For this, Vesery uses handheld rotary and reciprocating carving tools as well as fine-tipped burning tools. Finished vessels are dyed and capped with a turned rim. Some are gold leafed or even carved on the inside.

THESE ROUND BLANKS in a variety of wood species will be turned into delicate lips and rims for Vesery's vases, cups, and other hollow vessels.

A Neatness Fanatic

Vesery's shop is spotless. Machines are in perfect condition and tools are arranged neatly on the wall over his bench, with not a single wood chip hiding beneath it. Where most woodworkers keep cans of screws and nails with only general labels indicating their contents, Vesery's collection of fasteners is precisely cataloged and ruthlessly maintained. Individual storage bins, for example, not only list the size and length of the fastener but threads per inch and the material from which it's made.

He may owe some of his compulsion for order to the four years he spent as a navigator on a ballistic-missile submarine. Space on a sub is too precious to waste on an accumulation of junk. Whatever the reason, he can find anything he needs without fumbling—including the tiny screws he needed to repair the eyeglasses of an amazed dinner guest one evening.

Vesery's work takes intense concentration, but his role as a father also commands his time. With his wife working as a physician, Vesery is a stay-at-home dad for their two sons. When they are not in school, his children or their friends frequently open the door between the garage and house to check in. Vesery cheerfully answers their questions or settles a squabble, then the door closes, and he goes back to work.

VESERY'S FOUR-YEAR STINT aboard a submarine may have contributed to his highly honed organizational skills. Vesery's penchant for cleaning is well known among his friends: He once returned to his shop after a day's absence to find two garbage bags' worth of wood shavings strewn on the floor. The culprit was a friend who, as Vesery put it, was "just trying to get my goat."

For years, David and
Michelle have main-
tained a comfortable,
productive relationship,
each with a separate
work area but close
enough to nurture a
working partnership.

A Shop for Two

NOT A CONVENTIONAL
cabinetmaker, David ponders
how to fashion the limb of a
red maple into the stretcher
for a desk made from two
halves of a red birch log. He
characterizes his work as
"subtractive sculpture" and ex-
ploits the organic shapes of
crooked branches, hollow
stumps, and burls.

PPLEWOODS, a converted three-bay garage
that once housed a wholesale landscape nursery, does double duty: providing studio and
gallery space for married artisans David and Michelle
Holzapfel. Side-by-side woodworking is probably not
what they had foreseen as Marlboro College students
in 1970; at that time, Michelle was studying art and
mathematics, David Italian literature and language.

Although art was indeed in her future, Michelle was
not destined to become a mathematician, nor was
David ultimately to become a tweedy college professor.

ONCE A THREE-CAR GARAGE, Applewoods Studio has been the woodworking home of Michelle and David Holzapfel for 25 years. The 30-ft. by 32-ft. building, with a recent addition for storing wood, was originally used to house the equipment for a wholesale landscape nursery and is across the road from a shop where David Holzapfel apprenticed in the mid-1970s.

Instead, they merged their artistic interests in an unusually durable collaboration. Pursuing separate but parallel artistic careers, the couple has worked side by side in a shop they bought more than 25 years ago. "Nothing was planned in advance and then carried out," David says. "Rather, there was a draw, an enticement with the work and the material that initially led us to getting a shop."

A Little Luck

Although they are now well-established artisans, the road at first was uneven, even bumpy. David had worked at a furniture factory in nearby Bennington and, for a few months, in a small cabinet shop. By 1972, the couple had their first child. The following year, David started as a 75-cents-an-hour apprentice with Roy Sheldon who made tables from burls, spalted maple, and oddly shaped pieces of lumber. David wasn't getting wealthy, but on the whole, he found that woodworking paid better than writing poetry and translating Italian. Physical work also proved a satisfying antidote to, as he puts it, the "interior solitude" of writing.

When Sheldon got out of the business, it seemed logical to both David and Michelle to buy his remaining tools and supplies and go into business for themselves. "Logical but hardly practical," David says, "since we had literally no capital with which to do anything." But luck, hard work, friends, and trusting patrons intervened. A house and three-bay garage directly across Route 9 from Sheldon's shop became available. David and Michelle bought the property and launched Applewoods Tables & Treen.

A carver in high school, Michelle was familiar with tools and liked the process of woodworking. The couple bought a used Sears lathe on which Michelle learned the basics of turning, then she began turning table legs for David. She moved on to small vases and bowls. David eventually stopped using turned legs in his own furniture, and with their children in school, Michelle's career took its own path.

DAVID CLIMBS a fallen tree to harvest a branch whose shape has caught his eye. His work often combines the crooks and turns of material collected directly from the forest with the planed and polished surfaces of more conventionally made furniture. He confesses he often has trouble explaining to other people what he and Michelle do without showing them photographs.

MICHELLE USES a pneumatic carving tool, the work nestled in a stand she made from plywood and a tambour discovered in a salvage shop. The downdraft table on which she works was an early experiment in the Holzapfels' continuing struggle to control dust.

Parallel Paths

Although they share shop space, David and Michelle pursue their own projects. Indulging his taste for linguistics, David characterizes his free-form tables and benches as "a hybrid, a subtractive-rustico-AfroNakashima style." That is, he takes away material that doesn't belong until he is left with the piece of furniture that he originally had in mind. Pieces often start with the twisted branches of trees. When finished, they are often rustic in character and seasoned with African artistic aesthetics, the work of George Nakashima, or both. His work has been exhibited widely, and his clients now come from all over the country.

Michelle makes vessels, bowls, and other small objects that combine lathe turning with detailed carving. Intricate and highly individualistic, her work has won a wide following. In addition to a number of solo exhibitions, Michelle has placed her work in a number of major shows and both public and private collections, including the Museum of Fine Arts in Boston and the Smithsonian's Renwick Gallery in Washington, D.C.

THE TOOL Michelle most often uses is a small rotary grinder, held like a pencil. Starting with a high-school interest in carving, Michelle graduated to a used tabletop lathe after she and David opened their shop, and she learned the rudiments of turning. She later began to add intricate carving details to her turned vessels.

DAVID'S WORK ZONE, in the shop he shares with Michelle, is amply stocked with raw materials that would hold little interest for more conventional furniture makers. David only recently updated his side of the former garage with new drywall and paint, but his bench is still the mahogany base of a fire-damaged piano.

Michelle's finely detailed pieces have a sculptural quality: Wood is a raw material that she reshapes to enhance design. David is more likely to incorporate the irregular shape of a branch or burl in a piece of furniture without elaboration. Yet they have a shared enthusiasm for the potential eccentricities of wood—the burls and dogleg shapes of raw material overlooked or unused by more conventional furniture makers. "We currently call our business Applewoods Studio in order to convey that our work—each piece—is individual," says David, "that we're not cabinetmakers nor a production cabinet shop. Our processes have more to do with subtractive sculpture than they do with the joinery of more traditional furniture making."

Common History

Applewoods is the only shop they've ever had, and it bulges with the tools, materials, and experimental tinkerings amassed over a quarter century of work. Even with a 20-ft. by 12-ft. addition, which houses their wood supply and an air compressor, there is little room to spare. Their interests are wide ranging, and they tend to hang on to things.

Among their first tools were a handheld grinder and an electric handplane, both still in service. They inherited carving tools from David's great-grandfather, and for the last 20 years, Michelle has been working on a massive metal-turning lathe her father built to make kitchen-cabinet hardware when she was 13 years old. In the 1980s, David and Michelle switched to pneumatic tools, which they find safer and easier to manage than handheld electric tools.

UNHAPPY WITH the cabinet hardware he could buy, Michelle's father constructed this metal-working lathe when Michelle was a teenager. A 5-hp single-phase motor powers the 1,200-lb. machine, drawing 35 amps when it starts. Built from a mix of salvaged and custom parts, the lathe can turn either wood or metal.

Renovations at Long Last

Although the Holzapfels were steadily building a solid artistic foundation, resources were often tight when they began. Both Michelle and David remember fathers who were skilled with their hands, and when they become parents, the Holzapfels offered the same experience to their own sons. "They'd play there as we worked," David says. "We couldn't afford to buy them many toys, so they made them with our help."

There was also little money for shop extras when they began. For nearly 20 years, they labored in a dark work area whose ceiling was fiberglass insulation covered with plastic. They heated the concrete-block structure with a woodstove.

Then, a dozen years ago, the Holzapfels undertook their first major renovation. The woodstove was out, and in its place, they put in a gas-fired heater. Walls were rearranged, and windows were added to the showroom and to Michelle's work area. Insulation, drywall, and paint followed. They nailed up clapboards outside. A few years ago, similar improvements came to David's side of the shop. They decided, however, to keep the original

THE FINISHED WORK in the gallery attached to the Holzapfels' shop reflects an attraction to sculptural forms and free-flowing shapes, which have little to do with conventional joinery and cabinetmaking.

COLLABORATIONS IN LIFE AND ART

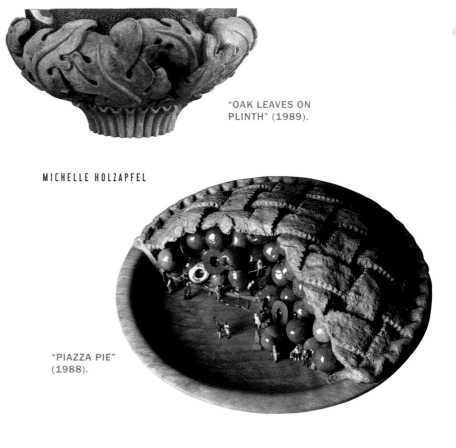

"OAK LEAVES ON PLINTH" (1989).

MICHELLE HOLZAPFEL

While different in both scale and intent, the work of married artists Michelle and David Holzapfel shares an appreciation for wood that is overlooked by mainstream cabinetmakers. Burls, doglegs, and hollowed logs are all fair game. David admits that both he and Michelle sometimes have trouble describing their work to people who ask about it. "There is the short form," he says. "We're woodworkers. We make vases, bowls, tables, and benches. And that's often the end of it." A longer answer needs illustrations.

Michelle's work combines both turning and carving, although finished pieces often look more like sculpture than they do a product of a wood lathe. David likes an African approach to art: The form of the wood itself is the starting point of design, a doctrine also espoused by George Nakashima (see p. 86). What is not part of the finished piece is subtracted.

Michelle and David's work has been shown in galleries and is in both public and private collections in the United States and Europe.

"PIAZZA PIE" (1988).

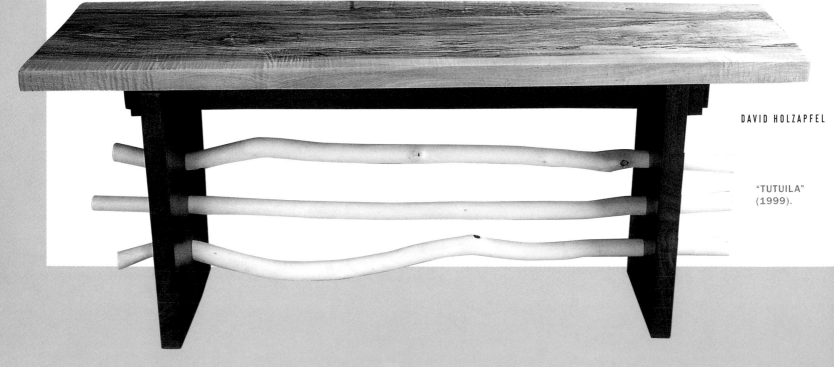

DAVID HOLZAPFEL

"TUTUILA" (1999).

"FIBONACCI VASE" (1991).

"SHELDON'S
WALNUT" (1988).

garage door in David's space. It allows him to move large objects in
and out of the building easily, and in the summer, he can leave it
open while he works.

Enhanced Collaboration

For years, David and Michelle have maintained a comfortable, productive relationship, each with a separate work area but close enough
to nurture a working partnership.

The arrangement allows them to stay close even as they follow different artistic directions. Michelle continues full-time at Applewoods,
supplying galleries around the country where her work is shown.
Arthritis, however, has forced David to abandon full-time woodworking. He teaches in a local elementary school and works in the shop
on weekends and over school vacations.

Their shop is still something of a cloister, and they've lost none of
their enthusiasm for the odd bits of wood that come through their
doors. "If a logger comes by with some interesting stuff, it's difficult to
say no," David says. "We've got enough materials to last us for at least a
decade at our current output." Old habits are hard to break.

HOLLOWED SECTIONS of a red birch log,
brought to the shop by a local logger, are as
valuable to David as a shed full of milled
lumber would be to a more conventional
woodworker.

ON A TRIP to Brattleboro, David came
across someone cutting down one of two
huge silver maples. Milled into lumber, the
tree yielded these slabs, which David stowed
for future use as benches, tables, or desk-
tops. Three years later, the same homeowner
gave David the second of the two trees.

"I want to give,
through my work,
some of that magic
wild kingdom I grew
up in where kids rule
and imaginations soar."

Time for Play

BARBARA BUTLER'S rented
shop in South San Francisco is
an 8,000-sq.-ft. space where
she and a crew of 12 build
brightly colored play structures for children.

NOTHING ABOUT THE EXTERIOR of Barbara Butler's South San Francisco studio suggests the vitality and exuberance of the work that rolls out its doors. From the outside, the building could be mistaken for the back of a plumbing-supply warehouse. But under its 22-ft. ceiling of arched wood trusses, Butler and her 12 employees build playhouses and forts for children, garden structures, theater and video stage sets, and a line of custom-painted furniture. Through 12-ft.-high doors out to a concrete loading dock, their creations emerge in brilliant hues.

Butler's first play structures were built onsite. She used her furniture workshop for storage. When she moved into a larger shop in the late 1990s, she was able to redesign her methods of work so she could make play structures modular and easier to ship. Butler's new approach allowed much greater control over her structures; the uncertainties of on-site construction and delays caused by bad weather were history.

Structures combine her love of sculpture, painting, and building, and most especially her love of play. Walls, floors, and roof systems are built as modular units, which can be put together in the shop, carved, finished, and then disassembled for shipping. Once onsite, her crew can pour concrete footings and reassemble the pieces. Even complex structures can be ready for use in a few days. Butler's approach has allowed her work to travel more widely than she might have imagined. In one memorable project, she and an installation team went to the south of France to build a variation of her "Rough and Tumble Outpost," a $87,000 collection of slides, walkways, and roofed buildings.

Basic Tools, a Vivid Imagination

There's nothing extraordinary about the tools or materials that go into Butler's structures. Her tool of choice is the grinder (she's still the only one who does the detailed carving). Cedar and lumber are the principal woods. Customers can order a structure from a list of stock designs, or they can work with Butler on a custom design.

This workshop, while large, gets its life from the people who work there rather than the space itself. Butler recognizes that it is the finished work that counts. "I have always resisted the urge to create the perfect shop because I needed to move in and get to work to pay the rent," she says. "I have seen lots of people start by spending tons of time and money fixing up their first shop. I think that's a big mistake because you don't know how you work yet."

AT WORK with her favorite tool, Butler decorates the entrance to a play structure in progress. She works with cedar and redwood lumber.

A STORAGE RACK along the wall safely holds trim pieces until they are needed for the final assembly of a play fort.

Adams leaps into the school year at a pace that would exhaust a marathon runner.

Man with a Mission

AN INSTRUCTOR WORKS at a bandsaw, one of three lined up against the wall of the school's huge machine room. Above him are shelves stacked with sheets of veneer.

WHAT COULD ONE MAN DO with a 12,000-sq.-ft. shop housing 18 lathes, 15 scrollsaws, four thickness planers, four jointers, five table saws, eight bandsaws, and 45 workbenches. Unsurprisingly, Marc Adams uses it to teach woodworking. His school, now about a decade old, is one of the largest woodworking schools in the country.

Adams teaches a number of courses himself but also brings in such woodworking luminaries as Bob Flexner, Colonial Williamsburg shop supervisor Mack

53

LEARNING TO CUT joinery by hand, a student wields a Japanese handsaw. A sign on the wall reads: "If wood costs $400 a board foot, what would your work look like? Pretend that it does."

Headley, Michael Fortune, Will Neptune of North Bennet Street School, Allan Breed, and Frank Pollaro, as well as toolmakers Thomas Lie-Nielsen and John Economaki and two dozen other professionals. Courses cover everything from basic tool use to joinery and design, veneering, finishing, and even metalworking.

SOME 1500 students a year enroll in classes at the Marc Adams School of Woodworking where they study everything from joinery to metal working.

THE EXPANSIVE machine room is well stocked with professional-grade equipment. While school is in recess during the winter, Adams builds furniture for himself and his family, much of it based on Disney® themes.

A Fateful Start

Although introduced to woodworking early in life, Adams had originally envisioned a career in sports medicine. But, while Adams was still in graduate school, he and his father went to a hobby and craft show and looked at a Shopsmith®, a combination woodworking machine. His father was enthralled, and Adams offered to split the cost of one with him. They picked it up on a Monday and assembled it on Tuesday. On Wednesday, his father died. Unable to part with the machine his father had envied but never used, Adams went to work making picture frames, doghouses, birdhouses, and anything else that would help him make the monthly payments.

His furniture-making skills improved, but Adams did not find a ready market for fine furniture in rural Indiana, so he veered into cabinetmaking. Almost immediately, his business prospects improved. He purchased his shop in the mid-1980s to house this fledgling cabinet business. Within four years, he had a thriving business with more than 30 employees. But then, not long after he turned 30, Adams decided to sell the business and move on.

A Turn to Teaching

Adams traveled through Europe on the woodworking lecture circuit, where he was stung by criticism over the laxity of professional training for American cabinet and furniture makers. And in truth, it was different than the old-school apprentice-

ships undertaken by European students, who spent years of hard work learning at the hands of a master before they ventured out on their own.

Adams began to perceive the1992 sale of his business as an opportunity to launch a school that would bring some of these educational ideals to the states. In the school's first year, a total of 160 students signed up for the 16 classes he offered. A decade later, Adams hosts 65 courses taught by a variety of visiting instructors and enrolls some 1,500 students a year.

By any measure, the school is a success, and Adams clearly enjoys what he has created. Adams leaps into the school year at a pace that would exhaust a marathon runner. During the school year, it adds up to roughly 90 hours a week. Overseeing this niche educational empire does not leave Adams with much free time or much privacy.

Winter Break

When the Marc Adams School of Woodworking is not in session, during the late fall and winter, the shop becomes a private work space. While his two full-time assistants repair machinery, disassemble and clean workbenches, paint the roof, and prepare stock for the spring's incoming flood of students, Adams is building furniture. "The other six months are mine," Adams says. "It's a chance for me to play."

And play he does. Adams can take as long as he likes on a piece. His particular interest is what he calls Disney furniture—pieces built around a Disney theme or movie. Many of them rely on intricate carving or marquetry, and some of the pieces have 1,000 hours of work in them.

During the school year, there must be days when October and the start of this six-month sabbatical look a long way off. If so, Adams doesn't show it. His perpetual cheerfulness seems to spring from a genuine satisfaction in the work at hand. Even at 4:00 in the afternoon, when most people are winding down from their nine-to-five lives, Adams is catching his second (or third) wind to begin a three-hour class on shop safety or joinery. He's a man with a mission.

STUDENTS IN a finishing class gather around Jeff Jewitt, one of many skilled instructors who teach the school's 65 courses every year. Visiting specialists include some of the biggest names in craft furniture making from both the United States and Canada.

STACKS OF dyed veneer stand ready for students. Shop assistants use the off season to prepare stock and equipment for students who will pass through the school the following year.

"When students leave here, they can look at almost any piece of furniture that comes through their door as a commission and know how to build it."

A Century of Teaching Excellence

STEVE SACKMAN takes a shaving from the rear apron of a curly maple lowboy, the last of the three major pieces he must complete to graduate from the two-year program.

ASK JUST ABOUT ANYONE in the narrow streets of Boston's North End how to find the North Bennet Street School, and you're likely to get a quick reply. "Right up the street," a man says without hesitation as he leans out of his car window and points. "Look for the place with the old clock." A large 19th-century clock mounted on the building at the corner of North Bennet and Salem Streets is as much of a landmark as the school's polished brass sign. Founded in 1885, the school is still in the same four-story brick

Benches are modestly sized and spaced so that students have just enough room to work. Classes run five days a week, from 8 A.M. to 2 P.M. When hands-on instruction ends in the afternoon, students are free to work at their benches until the building closes.

Classic Models and Skills

Students complete three projects during their 20 months at the school: a table, a chair, and a case piece. The school's bedrock principle is that students should learn with a "master," a highly skilled furniture maker (the school's instructors are also graduates of the program).

ALEXANDER RIOUX works on a mahogany candle box in "the incubator," the bench room where all full-time North Bennet Street students begin. The box is a prelude to the design and construction of a toolbox, a student's first major project.

Proposed by the student and screened by an instructor, projects range from small cabinets and stools to imposing secretaries. Each is drawn full scale before students begin work, a habit many North Bennet Street students take with them when they leave.

Much of the furniture that students make is patterned on Early American designs. There are exceptions, but these projects demand a full range of skills that, once mastered, allow students to build furniture in virtually any style they choose. Some students stick with furniture from America's 18th-century classical period, but many others develop more contemporary styles. "The school is not a design school," says Collins. "We're a trade school. We teach traditional methods of craft, and 18th-century American furniture just happens to be what most people will copy."

A SHOP WITH A LONG HISTORY

The building hasn't changed much in 100 years. The staircases are a little creaky, the doorways are narrow, and the wooden floors are well worn. The whitewashed brick walls are bearded in wood dust.

Although the surroundings are utilitarian, it's impossible not to notice the air of curiosity and productivity these rooms exude. Bench rooms are packed with half-completed pieces of furniture, tools, and lumber. At one bench, a student might be making a small cabinet with a beautifully curved door, which has been coopered and then veneered. At another, a student could be fitting parts to a Queen Anne chair or a low chest of drawers. In the drawing room, furniture parts and wood samples hang from the wall, while a bookcase houses three-ring binders filled with photographs of former students' work.

Woodworking machines—including an industrial-size bandsaw, table saws, jointers, thickness planers, and shapers—are relegated to an L-shaped room down the hall from the bench rooms. There is no snobbery about using machines to do the "heavy lifting."

Still, hand tools are vital and held in high regard by students and instructors alike. Students supply their own, and many somehow find the money for the very best. Passing through the incubator, Collins spots a $150 dovetail saw lying on a bench. She smiles. No one tells these students to spend so much money on tools, but they do anyway. They're in it for the long haul.

IN NORTH BENNET'S machine room, students not only learn how to use a full range of woodworking equipment but also how to tear it down, lubricate and adjust it, and then set it up for precise operation.

CHRIS GUNDERSEN works on a full-scale drawing, a requirement for all student-built projects. Sample parts hanging from the wall of the drafting room help students visualize possibilities for their own furniture.

What makes the shop especially interesting is not necessarily what is on display but what is so obviously missing. There is nothing that consumes electricity.

A Window in Time

AUTHENTIC DOWN TO his vest and a pair of buckled shoes, David Salisbury applies finish to a chair at the Colonial Williamsburg cabinet shop. The shop's eight cabinetmakers use tools and materials that would have been on hand in the original 1756 building, as they make period reproductions and educate thousands of visitors annually.

MACK HEADLEY and his fellow furniture makers might get more done in a day if only there weren't so many visitors. Yet they come by the tens of thousands, seven days a week, 52 weeks a year, to see a cabinet shop as it would have existed in the mid-18th century. Dressed in period costume—buckled shoes, stockings and knee-length trousers, white linen shirts topped with vests—Headley and his shop mates are glad to stop what they are doing and chat. They will, in fact, talk as long as you let them

VISITORS TO THE cabinet shop enter the building through a showroom where newly made furniture is on display. Pieces include a tall secretary, chairs, tables, and even a harpsichord, typical of the goods the shop would have produced just before the Revolutionary War.

about the tools and techniques that a furniture maker had at his disposal in the years just before the Revolutionary War. Better yet, they will show visitors exactly what can be made in such a shop: armchairs with graceful claw-and-ball feet, chairs with intricately carved back splats, elegant desks and tables, a harpsichord.

History Close Enough to Touch

The cabinet shop at Colonial Williamsburg is one of the few places in the United States where it is still possible to see anything like this. Even museums with the best collections of Early American furniture are, in comparison, lifeless exhibits; visitors there are separated by glass and rope from the objects they have come to see. At Williamsburg, furniture reproductions made in the shop can be handled. "Go ahead and open a drawer," one cabinetmaker tells a visitor eyeing a walnut secretary in the shop's showroom.

In the attached workroom, another cabinetmaker stands before a low workbench filled with examples of what the shop made and the materials that were commonly used: carved sample legs, a chunk of ivory used to make harpsichord keys, slices of ebony, and delicate fretwork for a Chinese-style table. Another cabinetmaker may be at work at a nearby bench. Outside, visitors may come across cabinetmakers as they make curved furniture components over an open fire. The experience is one of immersion for both visitor and cabinetmaker.

Reproducing the Past

There are 88 original buildings in Colonial Williamsburg—Virginia's capital from 1699 to 1780—and many more that have been reconstructed to their original proportions. Although a modern city with strip malls, gas stations, and motels has grown up around the historic area, the grounds are unsullied.

FURNITURE PARTS old and new line a bench in the cabinet shop's main workroom. Cabinetmakers versed in 18th-century tools and techniques turn out a range of furniture reproductions and, in the process, educate visitors numbering in the tens of thousands.

TO PUT A CURVE in a straight board, Marcus Hansen begins by plunging the wood into an iron pan filled with hot water. He and shop mate Edward Wright then clamp the board to a curved form and allow it to dry. Contemporary furniture makers use essentially the same process.

John D. Rockefeller launched the restoration in 1926, and Colonial Williamsburg is now a major tourist attraction. Headley's two-story cabinet shop is one of the reconstructed buildings. It was erected in the 1960s on the foundation of a shop that was built on the site in 1756. It consists of two rooms: a workroom, 24 ft. by 32 ft., and an attached showroom, 12 ft. wide and 24 ft. long. Heat is provided by a fireplace at one end of the workroom.

Staying Close to History

As the shop's supervisor, Headley manages both the work and the schedules for himself and seven colleagues. Cabinetmakers work 40-hour weeks, but because the shop is open seven days a week, Headley has his hands full keeping both furniture making and public education going at the same time.

BENDING WOOD for curved furniture parts at Colonial Williamsburg begins with a hot fire and a tub of water. Here, Edward Wright chops wood outside the shop as he prepares for a day of bending.

"I wanted to work with kids and was looking for a medium I could use that would reach them with things I really cared about. I saw hand woodworking as a way to do it."

An Inspired Shop for Kids

STUDENTS FROM one of Starr's woodworking classes pose in their shop with projects they have made. Students pursue projects that appeal to them, ranging from bandsaw jewelry boxes and canoe paddles to carved spoons and a miniature baseball bat.

A T 27 AND LIVING IN New York City, Richard Starr knew two things: He liked working with children and he liked woodworking, especially what could be accomplished with hand tools. At about the same time, a friend was singing Starr's praises to the Richmond Middle School in Hanover, New Hampshire, then one year old and seeking to start a new kind of arts program for its students. Starr, already certified as an arts teacher, applied for a job, the school hired him, and that summer he moved north to build

CREATIVITY, not per-fection, is the main objective in the New Hampshire middle-school shop classes that Richard Starr has taught for more than 30 years. Students like Genia Dubrovsky choose their own projects.

CARINA GRESSITT sands a jew-elry box whose parts were cut on a bandsaw by Starr. While stu-dents use a variety of hand tools and foot-operated tools, conven-tional workshop equipment is off limits. The approach has kept student injuries to a minimum.

what became the middle-school shop. In the fall, he welcomed his first class of students.

Traditional shop classes in many parts of the country have given way to "technology education," an approach that is both more aca-demic and broader in scope. Starr may be something of a dinosaur. He's sticking with sharp tools, lumber, and sandpaper. Yet his tenure at the Richmond Middle School has lasted more than 30 years, and his students are just as enthusiastic about making magazine racks and breadboards as they've always been.

Creating a Shop Culture

While in college, Starr stumbled across his future on a bicycle trip through Pennsylvania, running into a woodworker who made 18th-century furniture the old-fashioned way. His hand tools and spring-pole lathe fascinated Starr, and the experience proved to be the beginning of a career for Starr. "I wanted to work with kids and was looking for a medium I could use that would be a way to reach them with things I really cared about," Starr says. "I saw hand woodworking as a way to do it, to give kids hands-on experience with an interesting and difficult material and free some of their creativity."

It has become the mission and work of a lifetime. Starr's students, ranging from 10 years old to 14 years old, are now too numerous to count. There are as many as 14 students in a single 45-minute class, and Starr teaches five or six classes a day. Whole families have passed through his doors, not only siblings but the sons and daughters of former students. He now wonders when he will be seeing the granddaughters and grandsons of onetime students.

Starr has matched his teaching style to the skill level and interests of his students, detailing many of his ideas in *Woodworking with Kids* (The Taunton Press, 1990). Projects, however, often come from students themselves: stools, jewelry cases, bookcases, carved spoons, breadboards, tables, signs, boxes, and toys. The younger brothers and sisters of former students sometimes choose the same projects as their siblings, and Starr often takes photos of projects as a starting point for future students. "There is a shop culture because it's been around so long," says Starr. Some students have stayed in touch, and some have gone on to woodworking careers, including one local woodworker who supplies wood at no cost for some of Starr's classes.

In Plain Surroundings

Classes have taken place in the same 60-ft. by 25-ft. shop that Starr created in 1972 from a couple of ground-level classrooms. With painted cinder-block walls, a drop ceiling of acoustic tiles, and a gray commercial-tile floor, the room has no pretenses. Its last major renovation occurred in 1978.

The school district is planning a new school with new shop space for Starr and his program. He looks forward to more storage for student projects, better lighting, a dust-collection system, and just plain more elbow room. Yet Starr feels at home where he is now, and he'd be happy to stay put. To him, the program has never been about the space in which he's been given to work. That's proba-

NICK DOUGLAS works on a greenwood stool with a hand scraper, one of a variety of hand tools relatively safe for kids to use. His older brother had made a similar stool in one of Starr's previous classes.

STARR'S TIME-TESTED approach to teaching calls for equal measures of patience, encouragement, and genuine interest. A carved nameplate can be a rewarding start for a woodworker who's just getting started.

STARR TURNED two adjacent classrooms into a woodworking shop in 1972, when he left New York City and joined the staff at the Richmond Middle School. Although the last major renovation was years ago, the school district now plans to build a new school and a new shop.

BEN GRIGGS shapes a baseball bat on a foot-powered lathe that Starr built. Unlike a conventional treadle mechanism, this one is built around a bicycle sprocket that ratchets in only one direction. A push of the foot pulls a bicycle chain down to power the spindle; a return spring brings the foot paddle back to its starting position.

bly a good thing. With so many people using the same benches, tools, and equipment, Starr would drive himself crazy by worrying too much about his surroundings. It is enough that the program is still in place.

After the original remodeling project that yielded his shop 30 years ago, Starr turned his attention to teaching. And there it has remained. Ask him, for example, whether there is anything he especially likes about his existing shop and Starr is likely to give a one-word answer: "Kids."

Safe Tools

Some nicks and cuts are inevitable—Starr teaches a knife course, for example, and carving projects are common—but power tools are off limits to students. The shop's thickness planer, bandsaw, and table saw are Starr's exclusive domain: He cuts out the parts and students assemble them. Starr has, however, adapted two lathes and a scrollsaw so students can operate them by foot. The tools run at lower speeds than electrically powered versions, but they are safer.

Students also have access to a variety of hand tools: scrapers, spoke-shaves, planes, carving gouges and knives, handsaws, and egg-beater drills. One key tool in Starr's shop is an abrasive-belt sharpener, which allows him to resharpen dull tools quickly. "I've got to get tools out of kids' hands and back to them in 30 seconds," he says.

Looking for New Ideas

Although the basic focus and structure of Starr's class has changed little, Starr himself has taken classes that help him stay fresh or introduce him to new tools or techniques that he can later introduce to his students. Not long ago, he signed up for a two-week class on Northwest Coast Indian carving in Alaska and came away with new respect for the crooked knife, a traditional tool Starr describes as "amazing, spectacular." Safer than a straight knife, the crooked knife won a place on Starr's student tool list and has since opened doors for students who now carve with authority.

Starr has definite ideas about what helps young people learn about woodworking. Among bits of advice he'd give to parents: Don't worry if you're not an accomplished craftsman. It's important only to know a bit more than your child. A constant attitude of helpfulness is vital. Children need to know you will be there to help. Your attitude and your environment should express the thought: "This is a neat place where you can be safe, creative, and productive. This is going to be fun." Keep your frustration under control, he says, and remember that your unqualified interest is the key to success in working with children.

Even after three decades, Starr's interest in teaching other people about woodworking rather than advancing his own career as an artisan is undiminished. He keeps a small basement shop at home but complains that it is often overrun with debris or is used too often for household storage. When he has a woodworking project of his own, he usually uses the shop at school. It's easier, and in a way, the shop feels just like home.

A FOOT-POWERED scrollsaw proved more difficult to design than the lathe that Starr built. On a saw that originally ran using a small electric motor, Starr modified a freewheeling bicycle hub to increase the speed of the saw's up-and-down motion. Starr calls the mechanism "simple, safe, and surefire."

Homesteaders of the late 1960s and early 1970s were seeking a less complicated, more fulfilling way of life, and by all appearances, the Langsners have succeeded.

A Rural Teaching Tradition

DREW AND LOUISE
Langsner's 1974 purchase of a North Carolina homestead included this barn, which became the foundation for Country Workshops. Work areas are on the lower floors; wood storage and guest rooms, where students bunk during multiday sessions, are upstairs.

I N THE EARLY 1970s, Drew and Louise Langsner returned to the San Francisco area after a year-long scouting tour of Europe's rural corners. The couple had studied traditional handcrafts, timber framing, and log buildings. In an unplanned but pivotal apprenticeship, Drew had studied with master cooper Ruedi Kohler in the Swiss Alps. The Langsners settled in to write a book about their experiences (later published as *Handmade*).

 75

PUTTING PERSONAL fulfillment over personal gain, the Langsners have created a quaint and welcoming community where they live and work. Though born of necessity, sights like this aging barn-turned-carport have an appealing aesthetic in their own right.

They wanted to remain in the United States but not in the Bay Area. Homesteading in a more rural part of the country looked appealing, and with the publication of the influential *Foxfire* books, the Langsners suspected that the southern Appalachian region might be hiding the last remnants of the country's pioneer culture. In 1974, they found a 100-acre mountain farmstead in western North Carolina. It was exactly what they had been searching for.

Simple Beginnings

They knew from the start that they wanted to try small-scale farming and that Drew wanted to learn more about traditional woodworking. Beyond that, they had no idea what they would do for a living. So the Langsners began by writing magazine articles about gardening and woodworking, and Drew made wooden pitchforks. Three years later, through a visiting friend, they met Wille Sundqvist, a woodworker visiting the United States to coordinate a Swedish handcrafts exhibit in New York. Sundqvist spent a few days at the farm showing the Langsners how he carved spoons and hewed wooden bowls.

Sundqvist's stopover marked the beginning of a new career for the Langsners. Shortly after Sundqvist left, Drew wrote him a note: Why

COUNTRY WORKSHOPS' founder Drew Langsner meets with students in a chairmaking class. Proportion and shape give the chairs their characteristic stance, and attention to traditional green joinery helps them last.

MACHINES ARE welcome, even in a school where the use of hand tools is the core of the curriculum. Most students will use both as woodworkers.

not come back next summer and teach a course in carving Swedish woodenware? An invitation also went out to Peter Gott, who was asked to teach log-cabin construction. Both agreed, and by 1978 the Langsners had opened Country Workshops.

Since then, the Langsners' school has become as well known for traditional country woodcraft as the North Bennet Street School or the College of the Redwoods are for fine furniture. Course offerings have expanded substantially.

Drew teaches chairmaking, bowl making, and Swiss cooperage while a variety of other instructors/artisans teach subjects as diverse as bentwood boxmaking and Japanese joinery. One summer course invites a handful of students to learn kitchen and cooking techniques from Louise. Students live at the school while attending courses that last from two days to six days, staying in either a dormitory or one of several private rooms in a guest cabin or the workshop loft.

THE UPPER REACHES of the barn provide a storage area for drying lumber as well as two guest rooms where students can bunk while attending classes.

HELD SECURELY in a shaving horse, a chair post is brought to its final size with a sharp drawknife. The delicately faceted surfaces that result are a trademark of certain furniture styles, such as Welsh stick chairs.

CLASSROOMS AT Country Workshops are simple. The unpolished interior of the Langsners' barn/workshop makes a fitting classroom, where students learn to use spokeshaves, adzes, axes, and other tools of country furniture makers. Results like these two Welsh stick chairs, however, are anything but unsophisticated.

Plain but Serviceable

Interior spaces reflect the homestead barn's second life as a woodworking classroom. Workbenches are sturdy but plain. Floors are made from rough planks or unfinished plywood, and some walls are open to the framing. The 32-ft. by 48-ft. structure, built into a gentle hillside, has seen steady improvements over the years, including a 12-ft. by 28-ft. one-story addition, two dorm rooms and a bathroom on the second floor, and three separate shop areas on the first floor.

Its lack of artifice seems perfectly in keeping with a school where the subject is country and traditional woodworking. Students can learn how to make a ladder-back chair, carve a spoon, or hollow out a dough trough for the kitchen, but they do not travel to Country Workshops to make a Philadelphia highboy. Rural traditions are still the heart of the program, and while stationary power tools are available, Drew emphasizes the use of basic hand tools—the drawknife, axes, adzes, and spokeshaves.

His approach is carefully passed on to students. In one workroom, for instance, students can be found sitting at a line of shaving horses—a sort of combination chair and vise—shaping chair legs by hand with spokeshaves. Students studying green woodworking—making furniture from lumber that has not been dried—may start by splitting a freshly felled tree.

A Full Life

Homesteaders of the late 1960s and early 1970s were seeking a less complicated, more fulfilling way of life, and by all appearances, the Langsners have succeeded. They now offer dozens of classes in traditional furniture making and woodworking, passing along skills that are still useful and still important.

Yet money has never been abundant. The school was granted nonprofit status in 1980, making cash contributions tax deductible, and Country Workshops continues to call on volunteers to help with repairs and maintenance.

For Drew and Louise, managing the school and their own lives is a balancing act. It can be difficult. Shop space serves double duty—for Drew as well as his students—and there is a certain loss of privacy that goes with being resident workshop organizers and teachers. Drew admits they talk from time to time about moving, yet their homestead still exerts a powerful draw. "As I get older, I see myself as someone who teaches just a few people at a time," Drew says. "We like the small scale of the enterprise."

CLASSES MAY START with a log. Drew Langsner demonstrates the use of a froe for students in one of his chairmaking classes. Striking the tool with a rough mallet rives a section of wood, which can then be fashioned into a chair part.

A HEWING AX cuts a leg blank down to size. Although students have access to motor-driven lathes, many of the school's classes emphasize the use of hand tools and skills practiced by country furniture makers.

GREENWOOD CHAIR JOINT

Country furniture makers from the past often started with green, not kiln-dried, lumber. They learned to cope with shrinkage as the wood cured and discovered that it's not always a curse. Drawing on long tradition, Drew Langsner shows aspiring chairmakers how to take advantage of wood shrinkage to produce strong, long-lasting connections between posts and rungs.

The technique is simple and ingenious. A tenon in the end of a dry rung is cut to fit snugly in a mortise bored in a green, or nearly green, post. As the post sheds moisture, the mortise shrinks in size. If the wood used to make the rung is brought to an unnaturally low moisture content before assembly, the tenon will expand slightly as it absorbs moisture and reaches equilibrium with the

air around it. The two opposite forces acting on each other make a tight joint that will not loosen over time.

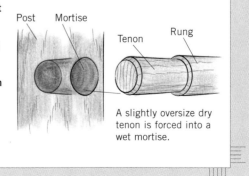

Post   Mortise   Tenon   Rung

A slightly oversize dry tenon is forced into a wet mortise.

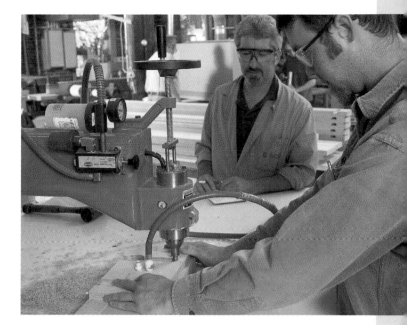

"The biggest challenge has been learning how to grow without sacrificing the values or the quality of the workplace we have created."

High-Tech on the Waterfront

AFTER SPRAYING on a catalyzed finish, Green's full-time finisher rubs out the surface on this table end to a satin sheen.

D OUGLAS GREEN'S THRIVING furniture-making company is the latest tenant in a 9,000-sq.-ft. brick building where the Portland Star Match Company did business shortly after the Civil War. Its high ceilings, exposed timbers, and bricked archways give it an urban warehouse feel, typical of buildings along the city's revived waterfront where restaurants and shops now compete for space. If the building has a faintly nostalgic flavor, there is nothing old-fashioned about the way Green works. Making

A CIVIL WAR-ERA match factory is now home to Green Design Furniture, a 9,000-sq.-ft. production shop on the Portland, Maine, waterfront, which turns out 500 pieces of furniture a year.

use of whatever technology has to offer is a priority, and Green thinks that's what's ahead for artisan woodworkers. "Love technology," he says, "wish we could afford more of it."

Furniture with Modern Flair

Green is a self-taught cabinetmaker who later studied industrial design at the Pratt Institute in New York. There is nothing small-time about Green's operation. The shop produces 80 different designs, including credenzas, computer desks, tables, bookcases, filing cabinets, bureaus, chairs, and sideboards—all in cherry and none with exposed hardware. Designs are reminiscent of both Shaker and Arts and Crafts furniture. Surfaces are uncluttered and clean. Tables, credenzas, and file cabinets often have sloping sides or heavily tapered legs. While there are a few exceptions, the lines on Green's pieces are straight rather than curved. The lack of any surface hardware and the use of

THE BUILDING may be old, but its arsenal of modern woodworking equipment keeps furniture production rolling. Green has fostered an informal atmosphere at work, but he also makes sure his crew keeps the shop clean and organized. "Every visitor remarks on it," he says.

GREEN'S WOOD of choice is cherry, whose pinks and tans mellow in time to a deep reddish brown. The shop currently uses some 37,000 bd. ft. of lumber a year.

elliptically shaped recesses in place of conventional drawer pulls give the furniture a somewhat minimalist flavor.

The shop where all of this furniture is made is also a blend of interests. Green manages 10 employees, including a full-time finisher and shipper, as well as furniture makers with a range of skill levels. "There's a lot of teaching here," he says of an operation that gobbles up more than 35,000 bd. ft. of lumber a year and turns out 500 pieces of furniture. Green also has been careful to preserve a small-shop feel no matter how busy they get. Employees bring in their own CDs for the shop's music system, and dogs spend the day lounging in their crates while their owners work nearby.

A Team-Based Production Line

Green spent years finding the most efficient means of moving work through the shop. Each piece in Green's catalog has corresponding patterns and templates that allow furniture parts to be made accurately and quickly. A three-ring binder—what Green calls a sequence instruction book—outlines each step. Small, self-directed teams of workers handle small production runs of a single piece—two beds, for example, or half a dozen tables—from start to finish. They move the furniture pieces through a number of "cells," groups of tools where related operations

CAREFUL PLANNING and a little flexibility make the most of limited floor space. Green's employees are invited to bring in their CDs, played on a shop sound system that manages to overcome the din of industrial-size woodworking equipment.

AFTER TINKERING with his approach to production woodworking, Green has adopted a system in which teams of artisans build small batch runs of a single piece of furniture. Once the furniture goes to the finisher, the team picks up a new work order.

AN INDUSTRIAL pin router is a key component of Green's production process. Held in place by a vacuum, a pattern guides a carbide bit as it cuts a furniture component to shape.

PATENTED INNOVATION

Douglas Green's patented assembly process relies on the sliding dovetail. It allows furniture to be shipped flat and put together quickly by the customer, without tools or hardware. The center stretcher assembly in this table connects the two ends. When the top slides into place, the table's components are locked in a unified whole that won't flex. Mating surfaces of the dovetail, still allow the wood to expand and contract seasonally with changes in humidity.

are performed. When these pieces are sent to the finishing room, the team picks up another assignment. Green's system takes the factory drudgery out of the process and has proved more efficient than a system in which a single artisan builds a single piece of furniture, an approach he has also tried.

After furniture assemblies are glued together, they are trimmed to their finished size on an Onsrud pin router, Dovetails are cut in a separate operation. Because Green's designs rely on extremely tight tolerances, industrial-quality equipment and careful methodology is essential. His pin router, for example, can be adjusted in increments as small as 0.005 in., crucial for his knockdown designs that rely on a precise fit between interlocking components.

"Most of the advice given to me by others was that I wouldn't be able to engineer solid wood to make it do the things I was thinking of," Green says. Undaunted, Green designed his system of joining furniture components with sliding dovetails. He holds two patents on the process. As a piece of furniture is assembled from flat components, each new piece secures the one before until the last part locks the assembly into a unified whole. There are no nuts, bolts, or screws. Furniture can be shipped flat, and customers can assemble a piece in a few minutes without tools.

Embracing the Twenty-First Century

Small shops that compete with high-volume factories usually look for ways to distinguish their work from mass-produced goods that usually cost a lot less. They may take longer to build a piece of furniture, rely on traditional hand-tool techniques, or build furniture completely to order. Green chose a different path, embracing some of the advantages of factory standardization even as he looked for ways to preserve the authenticity of craftsmanship. "What's interesting to me is how to use current technology to make something that is of its time," Green says. What he's offering customers, he says, is design and craftsmanship. He does not expect them to pay for any pleasure he personally would get by making a piece of furniture mostly with hand tools.

"I believe the next generation of craftsmen will be as comfortable programming a [computer-controlled] router as they are with a dovetail saw," he says. "The great question is whether the traditional craftsmen will adapt their talents and sensibilities to find expression with the new technology."

Green's approach has paid off, and although the business appears to be prospering, he has little interest in moving into a larger building or losing the flavor of his current operation. "The biggest challenge," Green says, "has been learning how to grow without sacrificing the values or the quality of the workplace we have created. Maine has a long history of talented, dedicated craftspeople, and we have had great luck in attracting the best."

UNUSUAL IN ITS USE of curved components, Green's side chair with arms includes a sliding lumbar support that moves up and down, allowing a user to adjust the fit.

> If most furniture makers bend planks of wood to their will, Nakashima looked for the piece of furniture waiting inside each board he owned.

A Woodworking Legacy

A DISPLAY AREA in the Conoid Studio showcases designs that made George Nakashima one of the nation's most influential postwar craftsmen. The studio, now an office for his daughter, Mira, overlooks a wooded Pennsylvania compound where the family still lives.

IT HAS BEEN NEARLY 60 YEARS since George Nakashima gained a toehold in Pennsylvania's Delaware River valley, not as the masterful furniture maker the world would later know but as a farm laborer who found himself chasing chickens. Born in Spokane, Washington, Nakashima had trained as an architect and traveled widely before he was held in an Idaho internment camp due to his Japanese ancestry during the early part of World War II.

GEORGE NAKASHIMA'S legacy is not a single workshop but a complex of buildings, which includes design and studio space, dwellings, a small museum, a structure devoted to finishing, and warehouses for the studio's enormous collection of wood. Although buildings are relatively close to each other, footpaths and careful landscaping enhance the parklike effect.

Nakashima moved East with his wife and young daughter in 1943, accepting an invitation to live and work on a farm that belonged to a former colleague. Later, he bartered with a local landowner for three acres of land. One small building became many, and Nakashima continued to buy additional property until he had tripled the size of his original lot and created a compound of workshops, dwellings, and storage buildings. Soothed by the hardwood forests and rolling farmland of Bucks County, Nakashima thought of his property as the core of his existence. Nakashima died in 1990, but his presence is still so strong that it is easy to imagine him stepping suddenly through a workshop doorway or emerging from behind a stack of lumber.

The Next Generation

Despite his death, Nakashima furniture is still being made. Nakashima's wife, Marion, and son, Kevin, continue to live in the house Nakashima first built on the property. Both wield some influence in shaping long-range plans and policy for the studio. But it is Nakashima's daughter, Mira Nakashima-Yarnall, who now supervises the studio and its workforce.

After her father's death, Mira wondered if the studio would fail. People who might have once ordered furniture assumed there was no one to make it. New orders declined. At one low point in the mid-1990s, Mira worried that if no one ordered a piece of furniture on Saturday—the one day of the week when the studio opens its doors to the general public—she would have nothing for employees to do when they arrived for work on Monday morning. Yet orders did trickle in, and in time the work backlog grew to a month or two, then several months. Now the studio is strong enough to keep 15 cabinetmakers, chairmakers, and finishers on its payroll, and anyone ordering a piece of Nakashima furniture has to wait a year to get it.

MIRA NAKASHIMA-YARNALL now works in the Conoid Studio, a bust of her father to her left and his indelible presence everywhere in the room. She assumed key design responsibilities a year before his death in 1990, marking out rough slabs of wood for individual pieces of furniture. The process, says Mira, "makes a Nakashima a Nakashima."

Wood as a Spiritual Medium

Nakashima worked in Paris for a year in the early 1930s and later on an ashram in Pondicherry, India, as the representative of a Tokyo architectural office. He was attracted

MANY OF Nakashima's designs revolve around live-edge slices of burls and roots, such as this massive slice of walnut against the wall of the Conoid Studio. In the foreground is the Conoid Chair that is still made in the studio's chair shop.

HONORING WOOD'S FLAWS

Reverence, even veneration, is not too strong a word to use in describing George Nakashima's attitude about wood. He bought whole trees on the stump and had them milled to his specifications. Then he stored the wood, sometimes for years, until the right project presented itself.

Thick tops on desks and tables, book-matched and left with a live edge, often were badly cracked. Rather than cut away the imperfections, Nakashima incorpo-rated them into finished pieces of furniture, spanning and stabilizing the gaps with wood butterflies mortised into the surface. Nakashima Studios, now under the direction of his daughter, Mira, continues to produce many of his original designs and to use what has become this signature detail.

After marking the rough location in chalk, a craftsman scribes an outline of the butterfly into the top with a scratch awl. (A) A router removes most of the waste, and a sharp chisel is then used to pare the mortise precisely to the scribe line. (B) Once the butterfly has been checked for fit, the inside faces of the mortise are coated with glue, (C) and the butterfly is tapped home.

The top surface of the butterfly, still protruding slightly, is planed until the two surfaces are flush. (D) The result is not only a hedge against further splitting but also a celebration of this plank's unique and natural character. "The tree's fate rests with the woodworker," Nakashima wrote. "In hundreds of years, its lively juices have nurtured its unique substance. A graining, a subtle coloring, an aura, a presence will exist this once, never to reappear."

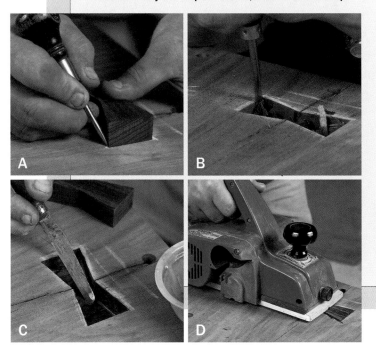

by the spiritual life of the ashram, and his career as a furniture maker blended a search for purpose with a deep attachment to wood and trees. Nothing, in fact, characterizes Nakashima's work as clearly as his willingness to allow wood to shape his furniture. Most furniture makers bend planks of wood to their will, but Nakashima looked for the piece of furniture waiting inside each board he owned, saving some planks for years until he understood their best use. He was an incurable collector of wood, not boards pulled randomly from the stacks at a local lumberyard but whole trees that he had milled into thick planks and put away for future use.

Mira says her father believed only wood and land were worth investing in, and he invested heavily: French olive ash, English oak burl, Carpathian elm, redwood, and walnut. The collection of wood at Nakashima Studios is still vast, occupying several buildings on the property. There was so much of it after her father's death that Mira was forced to leave some of it outside, and she considered selling it. Instead, she and her daughter designed and built a new warehouse, which, at a length of 140 ft., is the largest structure on the property. It is nearly full. Other buildings house smaller parts of the collection: virtual forests of dried timber that has been cut through and through and then hoisted into storage racks where it may mellow for years.

CONFRONTED WITH piles of valuable lumber painstakingly collected by her father, Mira Nakashima-Yarnall and her daughter designed and built a 140-ft.-long warehouse. The collection includes oak burls, walnut, and other species prized as much for their irregular shapes and swirling grain patterns as their mammoth size. Some of it is decades old.

CHAIRS ARE MADE in a building next to the Conoid Studio. This building was originally designed by Nakashima as a sort of clubhouse, a place where his woodworkers could relax.

BASES FOR DESKS and tables are often made from gently tapered rectangular components, which provide a sturdy foundation for more organically shaped tops. Tight-fitting joinery is essential since the strength of a whole piece may hinge on the integrity of just a few connections.

GEORGE NAKASHIMA designed the Conoid Studio with a thin-shell concrete roof that spans 40 ft. without any interior supports. Nakashima used the building, which gets its name from the shape of its curving roof form, as his design studio, as does his daughter, Mira.

Mira is still adding to the collection. She works with the former assistant of her father's logger, a man who tracked down walnut logs for Nakashima by knocking on doors and convincing landowners to sell the giant trees he had already located on their property.

A Continuity of Design

Nakashima Studios produces some 500 pieces to 600 pieces of furniture a year. Mira still makes furniture designs that her father pioneered, and she heads the studio in much the same way that her father did. Many clients visit the studio, not only to meet Mira but to help choose the wood that will be used in their furniture. Like her father, Mira sketches the rough shape of a table or desktop in chalk and later oversees the construction of the piece in the workshop. Although some components are made in batch runs to take advantage of the economies of scale, one artisan typically sees a piece of furniture through from start to finish.

Mira, who has lived on the property since 1970, assumed her role a year before Nakashima's death. Not long after suffering a stroke, he had uncharacteristically marked the wavy, live edges on a plank as waste, prompting one of the studio's veteran furniture makers to approach Mira in disbelief. The outline Nakashima had made violated every tenet of design he had established. "I realized I had to do the final marking because Dad couldn't do it anymore," Mira says.

Mira also produces her own line of furniture, which she calls Keisho, or continuation. A unique relationship between a single piece of furniture and the wood used to produce it remains at the heart of the process. "To me, that's the biggest luxury of this shop," Mira says.

You're in charge of it, from start to finish. You can actually go out and find these logs, go to the sawmill and watch them open up and see what kind of grain is in them, and imagine what they can be. People respond emotionally to the furniture, which makes it wonderful. It doesn't happen all the time, but when it does, it makes it worthwhile."

Workshop as Community

Nakashima Studios is not so much a single workshop or wood warehouse as it is a collection of interrelated buildings. "That's part of the thing that Dad was doing, too," says Mira. "He wanted to have an integrated environment. He wanted to have an integrated lifestyle." Workshops—a main studio for furniture production and a separate chair shop—are among 15 buildings on the property. Mira works in the Conoid Studio, a building her father designed with a thin-shell concrete roof.

A reception house provides overflow space for visitors as well as an authentically detailed Japanese tearoom. Down the hill is the Minguren Museum where both wood and furniture can be studied. Nearby is a single-story structure by a small pond that Nakashima used as a retreat. Footpaths link buildings and people to each other, melding the many parts of the studio into one.

Mira has been content to continue her father's work. Although she has her own style of furniture design, Mira has chosen to make no radical departures from the basic forms her father developed. Instead, she embraces a Japanese approach that honors tradition. Her own son, Satoru, has now joined the business.

GARY OHAMA works in the finishing room. The building is the last stop for the 500 pieces to 600 pieces of furniture produced in the studio each year. In keeping with George Nakashima's belief that finished wood should have a natural texture, the studio continues to use a tung-oil finish built up in multiple coats and then buffed.

Packed into a space roughly 18 ft. wide and 22 ft. long are the machines that allow Bradstreet to transform what is essentially scrap wood into something useful.

Making a Mark

ALAN BRADSTREET'S Pownal, Maine, woodworking shop has also housed makers of coffins and harnesses. Across the street, is a store where Bradstreet picks up his morning coffee or takes lunch with friends.

A LAN BRADSTREET'S SHOP stands by the side of a rural Maine road looking every bit what it is: a building with a story. By the time Bradstreet bought the place in the mid-1980s, the 150-year-old structure had already housed a succession of small-town artisans and tradesmen: a harness maker, a milliner, even a coffin maker. But before opening his doors as a woodworker, Bradstreet's first project was the shop itself. With a foundation of wooden posts, the shop had listed 6 in. to one side, and the front wall bowed alarmingly

95

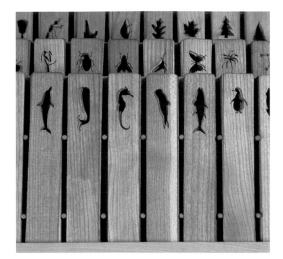

toward the street. With work, the shop regained its sense of balance, and Bradstreet took his place as its newest working tenant.

Assembly-Line Efficiencies

A single product leaves Bradstreet's shop—cherry-wood bookmarks—and he makes them by the tens of thousands. Each is precisely $\frac{1}{20}$ in. thick, $1\frac{3}{16}$ in. wide, and 7 in. long.

His highly specialized business has dictated his shop's tooling and layout. Packed into a space roughly 18 ft. wide and 22 ft. long are the machines that allow Bradstreet to transform what is essentially scrap wood into something useful. Bradstreet says a frugal Yankee upbringing and the sight of wasted edge trimmings falling from his table saw prompted him to make his first bookmark in 1986. All the wood he

now uses is recycled waste from larger cabinet shops. As a result, Bradstreet doesn't need either a jointer or a thickness planer, the heavy floor equipment that more conventional furniture makers use to turn rough boards into finished lumber.

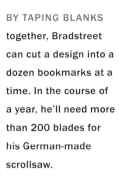

BY TAPING BLANKS together, Bradstreet can cut a design into a dozen bookmarks at a time. In the course of a year, he'll need more than 200 blades for his German-made scrollsaw.

On the first floor is Bradstreet's production area, and he relies heavily on just a few tools. A table saw equipped with a vacuum jig allows him to turn wood blocks into small mountains of thin blanks. An industrial-strength wide-belt sander reduces them to an exact thickness.

After taping a handful of bookmarks together, he traces a design at one end. Then he cuts out a pattern with a scrollsaw to form herons, leaves, penguins, palm trees, fish, musical notes, and frogs—130 stock patterns in all. In an upstairs finishing room, each bookmark gets a protective coat of linseed oil mixed with Japan drier and is readied for shipping.

A Fork in the Road

After a stint in the Air Force where he repaired electronic devices, Bradstreet went to work for a company in Maine that turned out wooden kitchenware: bread boxes, spice racks, storage canisters, and the like. What followed was a 10-year tenure in production woodworking that not only taught him how to manage a high-volume business but also gave him a deep appreciation for workplace efficiency. He discovered he was not, as he puts it, "a hand-tool purist." Quite the opposite. Bradstreet found the thrill for him was in devising ways to make a lot of things very quickly and very well.

After going out on his own in 1985, Bradstreet churned out small boxes and wooden desk accessories, gift items, and novelties—business-card holders, notepaper holders, clocks, wooden hats and bow ties, Christmas ornaments. Many of his products were in the $2 to $5 range. "I was the McDonald's® out there," he says, finding both fun and a sense of pride in what he could do. It was not a path many artisan woodworkers would envy, but it proved a perfect match for Bradstreet. Eventually, it led to a bookmark-only shop where he honed workplace efficiency to a razor's edge.

FROM BLOCKS of cherry, Bradstreet slices off thin strips that will be fashioned into bookmarks. A vacuum jig holds blocks securely and keeps his fingers safely away from the blade.

Carter inherited no family-heirloom tools, but her childhood provided indelible memories of a father who taught himself woodworking and carpentry.

An American Garage Classic

CARTER IS a long-time volunteer for Habitat for Humanity in Charlotte and is used to packing her tools for travel from one job site to the next. Her first shop, in fact, was her truck. With a larger shop, Carter has room to store tools for her Habitat crew. She gave crew members the combination to the lock on the door so they would have free access to the building.

IN THE BEST OF AMERICAN TRADITIONS, Anna Carter shares her shop with two cars, a fiberglass extension ladder, basketballs, her children's bicycles, a leaf blower, and a wheelbarrow. Carter, a volunteer for more than a dozen years with Habitat for Humanity in Charlotte, designed the two-story building and put it up with help from friends, family, local tradesmen, and her closest friends at Habitat. Her 320-sq.-ft. work space lies beyond one of the building's two car stalls. It's just a few steps from her backdoor and within sight of a backyard swing set she built last year.

LIKE COUNTLESS American woodworking artisans and hobbyists, Anna Carter shares her work space with the family car and truck, plus all the other odds and ends that go along with family life.

ALL THE BASICS are nearby in Carter's 320 sq. ft. of shop space. Work revolves around a professional-grade cabinet saw she was urged to buy by a woodworking colleague. She was wavering between the cabinet saw and a less expensive model when her friend asked: "You plan on staying in kindergarten forever?"

For the Simple Joy of It

Carter is not a professional furniture maker but a devoted amateur woodworker who is raising two small boys, does volunteer work in her community, and struggles to squeeze in shop time around a long list of pressing responsibilities. Carter learned basic construction practices at Habitat and says her furniture-making skills are still developing. "When people ask about my shop, I usually tell them I'm a furniture maker wanna-be," she says.

Her shop is used for everything from blowing up bicycle tires and repairing puzzles and chairs for her church's preschool to helping neighbors without workshops with their own projects: There have been popguns, skateboard ramps, a cypress box to house a wooden duck, and a pair of mahogany side tables. In a good week, Carter may steal 15 hours to work in the shop.

New acquaintances seeing the shop for the first time assume it belongs to her husband, Rob. But it is Anna who tinkers with tools and is slowly teaching herself how to build furniture by choosing progressively more difficult projects as she goes along. Although Rob teases her occasionally about her interests, he is also supportive, using birthdays and anniversaries to provide Carter with a steady supply of new tools. "He buys me tools," she says, "which is as good as he needs to be at this hobby."

Young Shop Mates

Carter's collection of tools and equipment would be familiar to any woodworker—a good table saw, a drill press, a portable planer, a chopsaw, a sturdy workbench, a jointer—but she has taken unusual precautions to make her shop a safe place for young visitors, including her two sons. They are encouraged to work on their own projects and to use a small bench Carter made for them.

The boys have grown up around tools, and they enjoy the shop. Carter says they can now "hammer as well as many adults." But she has a few unbreakable rules for any visiting children. When Carter is using a power saw, children must be safely in front of her where she can see them, and they must be still. She never leaves the shop without padlocking the main switches on two electrical panels. A single switch kills power at all shop receptacles. Sharp saw-blades are tucked out of reach.

A SIMPLE, U-shaped layout gives Carter bench and storage space along two adjoining walls and enough room for a larger freestanding bench in the center of the room. Windows overlook the backyard.

And in keeping with the discipline a small shop requires of its owner, Carter picks up after herself. "My brother-in-law, Joe, a talented trim carpenter, instilled in me that neatness was a partial ticket to safety and productivity," she says. "You use it, you put it back, and never spend time looking for it."

Gifts of Inheritance

Carter inherited no family-heirloom tools, but her childhood provides indelible memories of a father who taught himself woodworking and carpentry from books and, in the process, convinced her that self-education was possible with hard work. She remembers him as someone who made almost everything look easy and as a teacher who instilled in her the need to get it right.

Carter and her father made rabbit cages, added on to their barn, and built a darkroom in the basement. When she was 11, he showed her how to use a chalkline to make a perfectly straight layout line.

"My best memories of those projects were when we would go to Sullivan Hardware for materials in downtown Anderson, South Carolina," she says of her early experiences with her father. "It had high ceilings, oak floors, BB guns, lumber, nails, bits—everything you need to have a good Saturday. It smelled like old hardware stores used to smell—not antiseptic as they do now. It smelled of wood and oil, not plastic."

A DEDICATED floor sweeper, Carter is careful to clean up after herself at the end of a workday. She's a firm believer in keeping tools and materials organized and that neatness is a "partial ticket" to both safety and productivity.

"I'm fighting an uphill battle. There is so little quality left, but people want something in their lives that has meaning."

Shaker with a Twist

BECKSVOORT STARTED his one-man operation in 1985 and finished his 500th major piece of furniture before the end of 2002. Strongly influenced by Shaker design and tradition, Becksvoort builds one piece at a time and works by himself.

SIX YEARS AFTER he and his wife bought and renovated an 1830 farmhouse a few miles out of town, Christian Becksvoort was plotting a move to self-employment. He needed a shop. Behind the house, Becksvoort put up a 24-ft. by 40-ft. structure on pressure-treated posts and concrete footings, sinking them deep enough to escape the reach even of a Maine winter. At the same time, he accumulated both his tools and a backlog of furniture orders. By 1985, he was ready to leave his job at an architectural millwork shop in Portland and take up residence in his one-man shop.

THIS DELICATE music stand of Becksvoort's design is one of several un-Shakerlike pieces in his catalog. Of the dozens of catalog offerings, only three are exact reproductions of Shaker designs. Most of the others, while rooted in Shaker traditions, are subtle interpretations.

At Home in Sabbathday Lake

Becksvoort was smitten by Shaker furniture long before he opened his own shop. A 1974 trip to the Renwick Gallery in Washington, D.C., opened his eyes to the unique stylistic contribution that Shakers had made to American furniture. "That was the first time I'd seen Shaker furniture," he says, "and I just couldn't get out of there. I went back two or three times. It just blew me away."

His shop is close to the last surviving community of Shakers in the United States—at Sabbathday Lake—and he quickly established a relationship there. He offered to repair their furniture for free, which gave him the chance to examine it carefully in his own shop. Later, he built some furniture for the community.

Becksvoort's furniture has deep roots in Shaker sensibilities: clean lines, function over frills, and careful construction. Almost all of it is made from cherry, a wood species he knows so well he can accurately gauge the moisture content of a board as he lugs it up the stairs to his second-floor storage area. He makes one piece of furniture at a time, and he doesn't use plywood or veneer.

Becksvoort's catalog contains dozens of stock pieces, but only three of them are exact Shaker reproductions. Rather than simply copy, Becksvoort has distilled enduring Shaker ideals about furniture into modern pieces. His ability to interpret Shaker designs has brought him

HEAVILY INSULATED and heated only with a woodstove at the far end of the room, the shop stays comfortable through even a Maine winter. Windows on either side of the stove face a big vegetable garden.

clients from all over the world. "I try to turn out the best piece possible," he says. "My philosophy is not how cheap can I make it; my whole philosophy is how good can I make it."

Mixing Techniques

Well insulated and heated only by a woodstove, the shop houses both modern stationary power tools and a superb collection of hand tools. He surfaces stock by machine and swears by a Griggio horizontal slot mortiser. Yet any joint that will be seen is executed by hand. Dovetails are cut one at a time with a saw and chisel. He has cut so many of them, and they now fit so precisely, that he doesn't bother dry-fitting a joint before applying glue and assembling the pieces.

Becksvoort's hand tools are stored in a wall-mounted case directly behind his bench: an extensive collection of Lie-Nielsen planes, a

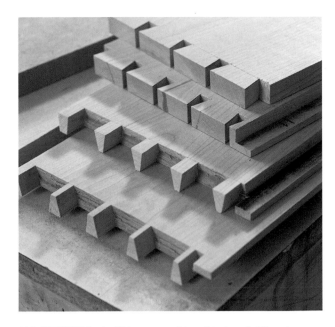

ALL JOINERY that will be exposed is cut by hand. After chopping thousands of dovetails by hand, Becksvoort no longer needs to test-fit the joints before he applies glue.

HAND-CUT DOVETAILS: MARK OF CRAFTSMANSHIP

Shaker craftsmen certainly did not invent the dovetail. It appears even in very old furniture and in Eastern as well as European designs. It is strong, reliable, and graceful in its simplicity and proportions. Possibly for all those reasons, Shaker furniture makers used it extensively. In a sense, it has become emblematic of their furniture and their approach to craft. Commonly used in drawers and casework where two pieces of wood meet, the joint gets its strength from interlocking pins and tails whose profiles are formed by hand with a fine-tooth saw and chisels.

Furniture makers these days often use electric routers and complicated jigs to cut dovetails. Once the boards are locked in place and the router is switched on, there is little chance for error. Yet there is no mistaking the look of dovetails that have been cut entirely by hand. Their proportions are finer and more delicate, and dovetail spacing can be adjusted to a board of any width. The process demands careful layout and exacting technique, and at any point along the way a slip of the tool or a waver of the hand creates a glaring mistake.

Either pins or tails may be made first, cut first with a fine-tooth saw and then defined with a sharp chisel and a mallet. The half of the joint cut first becomes a template for tracing complementary joints in the second piece of wood. Dovetails that have been properly cut slide together with some resistance—enough to ensure a tight, gap-free joint but not enough to split either board. Many furniture makers adjust the fit with a chisel before they dare spread glue and push the joint together—but not Becksvoort. He sits on a stool at his bench and chops out dovetails as if he were doing nothing more complicated than peeling an apple. When he is finished, he knows without testing that the joint will fit.

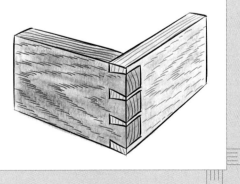

WHEN THE University of Maine no longer needed its card catalog, Becksvoort bought it for a song. It now houses screws, washers, ferrules, and other odds and ends. One drawer contains index cards on every piece of furniture he has made. They offer such details as dimensions, the length of time it took to build, the client, and the cost.

new set of Japanese chisels made by hand to his specifications, a set of well-used panel saws, screwdrivers, files, augers, and scrapers. Becksvoort, the son of a German cabinetmaker, is careful with his tools. He takes obvious delight in handling a prized plane or chisel; the usual clutter of a furniture maker's shop does not disguise an appreciation for order.

Like the Shakers, Becksvoort believes in thrift as well as organization. Instead of pitching the thin offcuts of cherry ejected from his table saw, Becksvoort cuts them to fit exactly in a small cardboard box and uses them to spread glue.

Wood screws, washers, brads, and a dozen other odds and ends are stored in the neatly labeled drawers of a card catalog he bought from the University of Maine library. One of the drawers contains index cards that offer details on every piece of furniture he's built since 1985: who bought it, how long it took for each stage of production, how much he charged. He finds the information useful in estimating custom orders. By 2003, Becksvoort had entered the vital statistics for his 500th major piece of furniture.

A Half-Hearted Wish List

Little has changed in his shop since he first built it. "If I had to do it over, I'd do some things differently," he says. "It still needs to be tweaked here and there. Other than that, it's a little more crowded, a little filthier but pretty much the way I had envisioned it."

A ROW OF sturdy bar clamps behind Becksvoort's glue-up table underscores his conviction that good tools are a better investment than cheap ones. He bought these clamps early in his furniture-making career and has never had to replace them.

There are, in truth, a few things on his wish list, such as a separate bay for wood storage. Lumber currently is stored on the second floor. Every one of the 500 bd. ft. to 750 bd. ft. of cherry he uses a year must be hauled up the stairs when it is delivered, and down again when it is needed for a piece of furniture. Becksvoort would also lay out the shop so he had a view of his driveway. Because the windows face a garden to the side of the building, visitors and delivery drivers arrive unseen at the shop door.

Becksvoort threatens a final change, this one involving one of the most intimate spots in any shop—the bench. Becksvoort works at a European-style bench that belonged to his father. It was made in the early 1900s, with a traditionally narrow top

BECKSVOORT'S collection of well-kept and well-used hand tools is housed in a wall-hung case of his own design; like most of the furniture he builds, it's made of cherry. The case hangs directly behind his bench.

and a recessed tool well into which tools seem to vanish. He'd like to replace it with a new one, something with a wider top and no tool well. "As soon as I build my new one, I'm going to donate this one to the Shakers," he says. Then again, he may not. The bench may have its shortcomings, but it is also hard to imagine Becksvoort standing before anything else as he works.

More likely is a continued devotion to making good furniture, without caving to furniture fads or to the pressures of making anything too quickly. His inflexibility on these points makes his furniture special and seems to underscore a philosophical connection with Shakers. "I'm fighting an uphill battle," he says, "I know I am. There is so little quality left, but people want something in their lives that has meaning, something that was made for them, that isn't off the shelf, that sets them apart from their neighbors."

Vocational school had given McLaughlin the basics of woodworking and hand-tool use, but it also convinced him that carpentry would be a life of drudgery.

Life on a New Hampshire Hilltop

SPACIOUS AND light-filled, McLaughlin's shop also has terrific views. In the winter, when the trees have shed their leaves, McLaughlin can see the lights of Concord 12 miles to the south. A steel tie rod took the place of a wood beam and allowed the shop's owner to make the most of a semicircular window.

TOM MCLAUGHLIN'S ROUTE to his treetop woodworking shop was anything but direct. It took him from a Massachusetts vocational school to the University of Lowell for a degree in mathematics, then through a three-year seminary program, and finally to Rocky Mount, North Carolina, where he was introduced to a man named Pug Moore. Vocational school had given McLaughlin the basics of woodworking and hand-tool use, but it also convinced him that carpentry would be a life of drudgery. In Moore's shop, he found something

111

far more appealing, a skilled furniture-making mentor who had run a successful business for more than four decades.

Moore was loaded with orders for 18th-century-style furniture, but at 73 he was slowing down. He had shed employees until he was running a solo operation, and by the time McLaughlin met him, his backlog of orders stretched out two or three years. McLaughlin asked him for a job. Although Moore refused to hire him immediately, McLaughlin persisted. He'd stop by the shop, and ask Moore to critique his work. Eventually, Moore relented. McLaughlin stayed for three years.

A CHANCE ENCOUNTER between Tom McLaughlin's father-in-law and the owner of a hilltop property in Canterbury, New Hampshire, led to an offer McLaughlin couldn't turn down. Renting workshop space from this owner allowed McLaughlin to return to New England.

PUG MOORE, with whom McLaughlin apprenticed for three years, kept these bedposts in his shop to show clients. Some of them still bear the paper tags he used to jot down customer preferences.

Accidental Encounters

The meeting with Pug Moore was the first of several serendipitous encounters—providential events, as McLaughlin thinks of them—that magically seemed to steer his life in the right direction at important crossroads. The next one landed him at an idyllic shop with treetop views of the New Hampshire countryside.

How that all unfolded is as complicated as it is unlikely. McLaughlin's father-in-law, a longtime summer resident of Canterbury, was in Massachusetts when he ran into someone who also happened to be from Canterbury. In the course of their conversation, the stranger, a man named Chance Anderson, mentioned that he had a woodworking shop. Would McLaughlin, Anderson wondered, be interested in using it? McLaughlin and his wife, still in North Carolina, were anxious to return to New England, and the deal was too good to pass up. So McLaughlin took over the top floor of a barnlike structure attached to Anderson's work-in-progress house.

Over the years, Anderson's compound had spread across a rural hilltop to include a house and a series of attached appendages that offered workshop space for McLaughlin as well as others. For McLaughlin, getting from his house elsewhere in town to his new hilltop workshop could be trying. Anderson's property is half a mile up a steep hill over a road that alternates between ragged asphalt and rough gravel. Still, there is a payoff in gaining the high ground, and McLaughlin has been able to pay off his rent either by making furniture for Anderson or by helping with projects around the compound.

Best View in Town

With windows across the entire southwest wall, the 1,200-sq.-ft. room that ultimately became McLaughlin's shop had ample natural light but not quite enough for Anderson. When Anderson bought the place, he added a barrel vault in the ceiling in the space above.

The changes make the most of a giant semicircular window in the upper part of the wall. On a winter's night, McLaughlin can see the lights of Concord a dozen miles to the south. In summer, he sees the leafy canopy of the southern New Hampshire hillsides nearby. Working at the bench with the windows thrown open to air and sunlight is one of summer's many pleasures.

MCLAUGHLIN LEARNED the fine points of his craft from a North Carolinian who specialized in 18th-century reproductions. McLaughlin's own work borrows heavily from the same furniture traditions.

Work in the Classic Style

One consequence of moving into Anderson's workshop was an excess of woodworking equipment. By the time McLaughlin took up residence, Anderson had turned his attention to stonework. He no longer needed the American® 36-in. bandsaw, the 12-ft. belt-run lathe, or his thickness planer. McLaughlin bought the bandsaw and learned to work around the equipment he didn't need.

McLaughlin continues to work in the 18th-century style, aided on occasion by templates and patterns he inherited from Pug's shop. While he appreciates the design sensibilities of Federal, Chippendale, and Queen Anne furniture, his own style looks more contemporary than the originals on which they are based.

New Hampshire has proved fertile ground for McLaughlin's furniture-making career. After returning to New England and settling in, he became a member of the New Hampshire Furniture Masters Association. This influential group of the state's top craft woodworkers

MCLAUGHLIN'S Conover®
lathe is portable enough to
travel for demonstrations. Behind it hang leg and bedpost
samples McLaughlin inherited
from the shop of his North
Carolina mentor, Pug Moore.

conducts an annual exhibit and auction featuring work in a range of styles, contemporary as well as classic. Along with the Guild of New Hampshire Woodworkers and the League of New Hampshire Craftsmen, the organization is responsible for elevating the profile of top furniture makers like McLaughlin as well as mentoring woodworkers still learning the craft. And that's the part of the equation that McLaughlin knows well. His own apprenticeship with an older and experienced master was a turning point in his career. He's only too glad to return the favor.

A CUBAN TALE

Tom McLaughlin is used to working with fine hardwoods, but hardly anyone gets a chance these days to work with *Swietenia mahagoni*—the fabled Cuban mahogany prized by 18th-century shipbuilders and furniture makers and now all but unattainable. McLaughlin, however, lucked into a whole tree.

The tree had died 80 years before he got hold of it and stood somewhere in the Virgin Islands before it was finally cut down. An American who had family living in the area obtained permits allowing him to buy and export the tree. It was shipped to North Carolina where it was cut into veneer, then trucked to California where it was stored as the owner searched for a buyer.

McLaughlin and fellow New Hampshire furniture maker David Lamb could get the best price by buying the entire tree's worth of veneer, but at $28,000, it was beyond their reach. Their novel idea was to sell "shares" in the wood, offering furniture customers a chance to buy some of the veneer for future use. They raised enough cash to make the purchase, assuring themselves and their customers of a supply well into the future. One of these pieces was this game table.

"My way of looking at it is that in a fine cabinet shop the heart of it all is a table saw, so we wanted to invest in a very good one. We spent half of our original money on that."

Keeping Arts and Crafts Alive

ROOF TRUSSES (made on site and lifted into place by a crane) keep the floor area free of supporting posts and columns, and a ceiling more than 11 ft. high makes the space airy and filled with light. Both Rodel and Mack work at their own benches at one end of the shop, a shared table saw between them.

KEVIN RODEL AND SUSAN MACK, partners in woodworking as well as in marriage, were urban refugees looking for a quiet country life when they left Philadelphia in the late 1970s. They found the lifestyle they wanted in Maine, but there was still the question of making a living. Kevin lasted a single day at a fish-packing plant in Yarmouth and then picked up work wherever he could find it. Eventually the couple both landed something steady at L.L. Bean, the Maine-based outdoor clothing and equipment retailer.

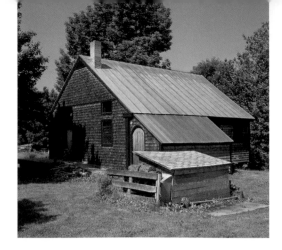

BUILT ON a shoestring, the Maine workshop of Kevin Rodel and Susan Mack reflects the same attention to detail that has characterized their Arts and Crafts furniture. Thick insulation, well-made windows, and a standing-seam metal roof all have contributed to a comfortable working environment.

RODEL'S STINT in a local timber-framing company is evident in the timber frame of the shop. Traditional joinery includes touches like the lamb's tongue transitions between the square edge and chamfer at the post corners and the pegged scarf joint in the beam above.

It would be another year before the team of Mack & Rodel, as their furniture-making venture would later be called, became full-time woodworkers at Thomas Moser, then a fledgling furniture company housed in a converted Grange Hall. When Moser decided to expand, Mack and Rodel decided to move on. But by then, work was already underway on their own shop.

Building a Smart Shop

They chose a spot on the edge of a clearing not far from the 19th-century fixer-upper they had bought on 40 acres of fields and forest. Working mostly by themselves, with help now and then from friends and neighbors, Mack and Rodel started with a foundation of concrete piers and site-built beams.

They bought 2-in. spruce floor planks from a local lumberyard and sheathed the inside walls with horizontal boards. They built roof trusses on the site, designing them so the shop's interior would be free of supporting posts. Two years later, they had a comfortable shop: an open, light-filled space 32 ft. by 26 ft., with a ceiling of nearly 11½ ft. They installed two matching workbenches where they pursued their own furniture projects.

Hiring out as little of the construction to outside contractors as possible helped the couple afford to build a shop. And careful planning has paid off in low operating costs. Fluorescent lighting and efficient 220-volt power tools have kept combined power bills for home and shop to about $70 a month. Heat comes solely from an airtight woodstove, which is capable of running through the night. Because Mack and Rodel insulated the building carefully and invested in well-made windows, they stay warm with less than three cords of wood a year—a pittance by Maine wood-heating standards.

PHOTOGRAPHS and postcards tacked inside Kevin's wall-mounted tool cabinet reflect his devotion to the Arts and Crafts tradition, as well as to modern interests such as the unexpectedly subtle observations of cartoonist Bill Watterson's Calvin and Hobbes.

QUARTER-SAWN ADVANTAGE

Quartersawing white oak (slicing the wood so its growth rings are perpendicular to the face of the board) unveils dramatic, almost startling, rays in the wood's structure. Abundant, strong, and visually lively, white oak became a favorite of the Arts and Crafts movement. It remains a primary choice for contemporary craftsman working in Arts and Crafts designs. One of the reasons for its continued popularity, says Rodel, is that it can take on a range of colors without losing the distinctive patterns of its grain and figure.

There are practical advantages, too. Quartersawn lumber is less likely to cup or warp than flatsawn wood. Dimensional changes caused by seasonal fluctuations in humidity are far less pronounced than they are in flatsawn material. That makes the wood ideal for tabletops and door panels as well as closely fitting parts such a drawer sides.

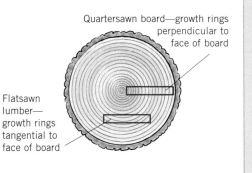

Quartersawn board—growth rings perpendicular to face of board

Flatsawn lumber— growth rings tangential to face of board

A time-tested recipe for coloring quartersawn white oak is by fuming it with a strong solution of ammonia. Unlike liquid stains, fuming leaves no residue that can choke the pores of the wood. Final wood tones are dictated by the length of time the wood remains in the fuming chamber—from a slightly darkened surface with a few hours of exposure to the deep browns that emerge from an overnight stay.

Because the effect of ammonia varies, Rodel tests samples of lumber in a chamber before committing a finished piece of furniture. When he's done, all that remains is to apply a final coat of linseed oil. It's rubbed on in thin coats that dry to a soft, protective sheen.

Although amenities are few, there is running water thanks to a device called a yard hydrant—a hand-powered spigot atop a galvanized pipe that disappears through the floor just to the left of their sharpening station. The shop, in fact, was carefully located to take advantage of a buried water line running between their well and the house.

Investing Wisely

Mack and Rodel were just as prudent in the selection of their tools as they were in building the shop. Two old-timers—a small, prewar

THE COUPLE devoted half their tool budget to a precision table saw, but a well-engineered sliding table, adjustable fences, and an integral mortising machine made it a sound investment. Behind Kevin is the shop's source of water: a yard hydrant that taps into a water line buried beneath the building.

Delta® bandsaw bought at auction before leaving Philadelphia and a 1920s' belt-driven drill press made by Canedy-Otto—continue to serve faithfully. The drill press is an especially beautiful piece of equipment with an arched neck and counterbalanced quill.

Mack and Rodel also spent money for top-quality new equipment where it mattered. In the center of the shop is a combination horizontal mortising machine and table saw made by Ulmia. It cost them $6,000—when there was hardly $6,000 to spend. "My way of looking at it is that in a fine cabinet shop the heart of it all is a table saw, so we wanted to invest in a very good one," says Rodel. "We spent half of our original money on that." Its precision and durability has more than repaid the debt.

From Shaker to Mackintosh

Mack and Rodel's six years at Thomas Moser was an immersion in Shaker furniture. At the time, the company employed six cabinetmakers, each with his or her own bench and the responsibility for a piece of furniture from start to finish. One of their old bench mates, Christian Becksvoort, went on to start his own shop just a few miles down the road. He still specializes in Shaker-inspired designs (see p. 104).

Mack and Rodel found themselves drawn, however, to Arts and Crafts furniture. They saw something deeply appealing about the early work of Frank Lloyd Wright, Charles Limbert, Greene and Greene, and maybe most of all, the Scottish designer Charles Rennie Mackintosh. It felt particularly natural to Rodel. He began designing his own furniture in that style, and he now does nothing else. Careful workmanship, precise joinery, and a fumed finish on quartersawn white oak characterize his work. His backlog of orders goes out two years. "I'm surprised they will wait that long," Rodel says. "But they do."

There have been other changes as well. The couple now has two sons, and Mack serves on the town's Board of Selectman, the community's governing body. Town business keeps her from working in the shop, making Mack & Rodel essentially a solo operation. Mack helps in a crunch, but her full-time days at the bench next to Rodel's have ended for now.

KEVIN RODEL spent years working in a shop that made Shaker designs, but he later drifted toward Arts and Crafts designs, particularly the work of Charles Rennie Mackintosh, an influential Scottish designer.

THIS SIDE CHAIR in quartersawn white oak with a green leather seat is typical of the Arts and Crafts–style furniture at the core of Kevin Rodel's furniture-making interests.

"I started out as an expert and then spent years discovering how much I didn't know."

A Country Character

JACOB CRESS'S shop is a 1784 log cabin adjoining the house that he and his wife, Phebe, bought in Fincastle, Virginia. Although Cress nearly doubled its size by building an addition for stationary power tools, the original 16-ft. by 24-ft. cabin is still at the heart of his furniture-making venture.

I T WAS JACOB CRESS'S WIFE, Phebe, who found the 1830 brick house with its Victorian wing in Fincastle, Virginia, in the late 1970s. When Cress asked whether the new place had room for a shop, she told him there was a cabin out back that might do. It did just fine, and Cress learned that, in fact, the cabin's previous owner had himself been a woodworker. Cress felt right at home, and for the last 20 years, he has been producing both reproduction and highly original work in this one-story log cabin originally built in 1784. In this

CRESS HAS done little to change the appearance of the 18th-century log cabin he uses as a shop. Other than rewiring the building and repairing gaps between the logs with mortar, Cress was content with the building's condition when he moved in 20 years ago.

community of fewer than 400, Cress is more than the local furniture maker. A former Navy submariner who once pondered a career in acting, Cress is a genuine iconoclast who, along with more traditional commissions, takes pleasure in creating nonconformist furniture based on classic 18th-century styles.

First Real Shop: An Old Mill

Cress, now in his mid-50s, came to full-time furniture making on a long, elliptical path. Shortly after leaving the navy in 1969, a flat-broke Cress decided to make a set of tables as a wedding gift for his only brother. With not much more than a handsaw and a clamp improvised from a car jack, Cress jumped into the project. A few years later, he teamed up with his brother to open a woodworking business in Abingdon, Virginia, where Phebe ran an antique shop.

A year later, the couple moved to the country, taking over a three-story mill more than a century old, where Cress launched his solo furniture career. It was no easy task. Miles from a town of any size, without money to pay for advertising, and with little business experience, Cress found furniture commissions few and far between.

Shop and home were one, and the mill's 3-ft.-thick stone walls made the winters long and cold. But Cress worked at it. Aided by Phebe's knowledge of 18th-century furniture styles, Cress became a skilled restorer and maker of furniture reproductions, and he steadily expanded his client list. Later, when he and Phebe moved to Fincastle, Cress was already well established as a competent, if traditional, furniture maker.

CRESS GIVES a final polish to a mahogany table patterned loosely after a Philadelphia Chippendale design. One key difference: A mouse peers from an opened Lamp of Wisdom on the front apron. In the background is a Chinese Chippendale-style occasional table.

A New Home in Fincastle

Cress's new cabin workshop, just a few steps from his back door, needed chinking and new wiring before he could move in. Cress built an addition to the original tin-roof cabin, nearly doubling its 16-ft. by 24-ft. footprint. The addition provides machine space and a back porch overlooking a small pond and waterfall, where Cress does his carving. Yet the cabin is still the heart of the shop, even though it's not designed for high-production work.

This suits Cress because he isn't interested in turning out mountains of furniture. Each piece gets his undivided attention, and he works slowly. He starts with conventional shop equipment—planer, table saw, lathe—but after milling rough lumber by machine, Cress turns to hand tools. His furniture is beautifully detailed with all the authority and presence of the originals on which they are based. As his furniture-making repertoire broadened, Cress also realized there was far more to learn than he had imagined at the start. "I started out as an expert," he says, "and then spent years discovering how much I didn't know."

Furniture Classics with a Twist

After years of conventional furniture making, Cress took an important step in 1990, creating his first "animated furniture." The piece is a Philadelphia Chippendale chair he named "Oops!" It has the classic lines of a Chippendale, the same graceful back, the curving crest rail, the claw-and-ball feet—all of the right ingredients. But there is a difference. The ball in one front leg has managed to escape, and the chair's leg is reaching to recapture it. A pair of wide eyes embedded in the chair's back splat watch the scene unfold. Intended to poke fun at overly serious galleries and artisans, the chair landed on the back cover of *Fine Woodworking* magazine. Since then, Cress has produced a series of like-minded pieces. His Chippendale series also includes a piece whose arms clutch chisel and mallet to allow the chair to carve its own knee.

Making furniture like this is more difficult than reproducing the originals. Furniture parts that would normally be straight must twist or bend to become arms and legs in motion. The work is challenging, and it helps Cress make a point: Don't take life too seriously.

PATIENCE AND a steady hand helped Cress learn how to produce 18th-century detailing like this Lamp of Wisdom and the hand-carved gadrooning below it. An urge to deflate overblown gallery rhetoric produced the mouse.

INSPIRED BY an Al Hirschfeld drawing in which the artist was drawing himself, Cress produced in walnut this Chippendale chair that watches as it carves its own knee. Cress calls the work "Self Portrait."

"It's hard to make a living out here in the mountains, but I love woodworking so I started a shop on a very small basis—and then expanded it."

Wyoming Mountain Retreat

WHAT HAD BEEN a two-bay garage became the heart of Rawlings's shop, a good start but not enough to house a growing woodworking business. The low addition on the right, used as a spray-finishing and bench room, replaced a greenhouse.

THE VIEW FROM DON RAWLINGS'S shop window takes in more than the mountain scenery of Wyoming's remote Absaroka Range some 40 miles northwest of Cody. He might look up to see a herd of elk or a knot of grizzly bears in the valley below his house. For Rawlings, the early-morning panoramas are as inspiring as they are removed from the flat Ohio countryside where he grew up and began a career in banking. When he moved his family to Wyoming more than 20 years ago, access to their homestead was by dirt

HARD WORK and self-reliance helped Rawlings create tools as well as rolling- and wall-mounted storage cabinets, when there wasn't enough money to shop in catalogs. He designed and built the ambient air cleaner suspended from the ceiling.

WYOMING'S REMOTE Sunlight Basin in the mountains northwest of Cody is the backdrop for Don Rawlings's shop, a total of 2,000 sq. ft. occupying part of the ground floor of his house and a detached, two-story building nearby.

road. Now there is a paved state highway, and neighbors are a little closer than they used to be. Yet, by nearly any definition, Rawlings's surroundings are still pristine.

Building a Homestead

"It's hard to make a living out here in the mountains," Rawlings says, "but I love woodworking so I started a shop on a very small basis, doing anything—kitchen cabinets, furniture, whatever—and then expanded it." Rawlings, his wife, and three sons built their homestead slowly, hauling water from a nearby creek and buying lumber locally from a sawmill. "It was kind of the pioneer way, the old-fashioned way," he says.

Rawlings's woodworking began with a miscellaneous collection of hand tools and no dedicated shop space until he graduated into what had been a two-bay garage beneath his house. Later, he dismantled an adjacent sunroom and replaced it with a 480-sq.-ft. shop addition that became a finishing room. Eventually, his growing business prompted him to build a freestanding 800-sq.-ft. building nearby that now houses a machine shop on its first floor and a storage and assembly area upstairs. In all, Rawlings has some 2,000 sq. ft. of shop space under roof.

An Imaginative Self-Reliance

Rawlings describes himself as both particular and orderly, and his shop space bears him out. A cabinet saw flanked by two router tables dominates the center of the main shop, while custom-built storage and work carts are on casters to allow more flexibility in managing workflow. Oak storage cabinets lining the walls above his workbenches may look like kitchen-cabinet castoffs, but Rawlings built them especially for the space. On one wall, a pair of double-hinged doors swing open to reveal a capacious storage area packed with staples, nails, and screws that would rival the collection of a modest hardware store.

Many of the amenities Rawlings has built into his work space are homemade, including a spline-mortising machine he designed and built for face-frame work and two pneumatically controlled router shapers. "We don't have a ton of money in fancy tools and jigs and all these things you see in the magazines and the woodworking catalogs," Rawlings says. "We just kind of make our own as we go and do what we need to do."

Not a Banker's Life

He came by his habits honestly. His father, also an Ohio banker, once made a room full of storage built-ins from a pile of fish crates he picked up. Each one had to be taken apart, thoroughly scrubbed and sanded and then put back together. He may have watched his father work at home, but Rawlings was not encouraged to use his father's tools.

DOUBLE DOORS on full-length piano hinges unfold to reveal a roomy storage cabinet where Rawlings has packed his extensive collection of fasteners (below). Above the cabinet is an ornamental coat of arms left over from a house decorating job years ago that Rawlings hung up rather than toss out (above).

RAWLINGS CONFESSES he is not as tidy as he used to be, but bins of scrupulously organized nuts and bolts would still be the envy of many other woodworkers. He once carried this neatly packed case on cabinet and restoration work that took him away from his shop.

SEEING A NICHE and learning that a potential rival was going out business, Rawlings launched Stage West to make a line of trunks and cabinets styled on 19th-century designs.

Later, when his interest in woodworking started to unfold and he had sons of his own, Rawlings made sure they each had a bench and tools. "I vowed to let them do, create, and learn," he says, and the effort paid off. All of them have ended up somewhere in the building trades. One is a construction engineer, another a cabinetmaker and finish carpenter for high-end houses springing up nearby, and the third is with Habitat for Humanity in Africa.

Rawlings gets occasional help from his wife and oldest son, but mostly his work is a solo experience punctuated only by intermittent holidays. He does not, he says, encourage social interruptions.

A New Direction

Like many other furniture makers before him, Rawlings learned a great deal by making mistakes. A 14-ft. rosewood conference table he built on commission, for example, delaminated after the contact cement he used to anchor the veneer failed. It was a temporary setback, and Rawlings went on to run a successful niche business making trunks. Once a staple of travelers who packed for long holidays, steamer trunks had largely disappeared. But Rawlings found plenty of people who still wanted them. Customers of Stage West found plenty of uses for Rawlings's trunks and cabinets. They went to horse barns for storing tack, to houses where they were used as storage cabinets, and even onboard boats. Rawlings made them in the 19th-century style out of oak, cherry, and walnut and offered any exotic veneer a customer asked for. He lined them with aromatic cedar and bought heavy brass hardware from a company that had been in business for nearly 150 years.

While Rawlings still makes trunks, his interests have widened to include western-themed art furniture, like the limited edition "Nez Perce," a storage cabinet covered in suede leather and decorated with traditional beads, antler pieces, and tin cones. It is named for the Indian leader Chief Joseph, whose retreat from the U.S. Army took him through the valley where Rawlings now lives. For the last four years, Rawlings's work has been featured in the sourcebook of the Western Design Conference, a collection of work by regional artisans.

The Thrill Is Never Gone

More than 40 years in a woodworking shop has not left Rawlings unscathed: Serious arthritis has crippled his hands, and spray-finishing without a respirator, along with other self-described bad habits, has left him with pulmonary fibrosis. It has been enough to slow him down slightly but not enough to force him to quit. He rises at 6 A.M. to make espresso and is in his shop well before a bank officer would typically be starting work.

Rawlings has lost little of his enthusiasm for the woodshop. He still considers it a sanctuary, which has been more than a place simply to earn a living. "The shop has been a great experience for all of us," he says. Even now, Rawlings says there is still nothing as pleasing as walking in and picking up the scent of walnut or oak shavings still in the air from yesterday's work. "To walk into any shop and smell these smells, to hear the swoosh of a handplane, and to see stickered piles of lumber gives me goose bumps," he says. Age and ill health has done nothing to change that.

Wiley appreciates the solitude his property and workshop afford, finding them an ideal environment for incubating new carving and furniture designs.

High Art in the High Desert

AN OUTDOOR STRUCTURE between Wiley's house and shop offers 160 sq. ft. of shade on a hot summer afternoon. Wiley framed his gazebo with railroad ties for corner posts and aspen logs for roof beams, but with rain so infrequent, he never found the need to cover the roof sheathing with shingles.

TWENTY-FIVE YEARS AGO, all James Wiley had in mind was a place to open a small-engine and chainsaw repair shop on the outskirts of Taos, New Mexico. A 12-ft.-sq. chicken coop 20 yards from his house looked ideal, and after coaxing his flock to a new pen, Wiley moved in his equipment. It was the start of a process that ultimately would transform Wiley from a small-engine mechanic to a full-time woodcarver and furniture maker with enough work to keep him busy 70 hours a week. His tiny chicken coop has grown, too,

A LOVE FOR CARVING

Wiley's devotion to carving began with simple Hispanic designs but soon grew to include more sophisticated patterns influenced by European as well as regional artists. His work has appeared in local and statewide exhibitions, and other woodworkers often ask for his advice on Territorial-style architectural detailing. Self-taught in both carving and furniture making, Wiley combines his skills in chairs, casework, and cabinetry. Since abandoning small-engine repair, Wiley has built a busy woodworking and carving business. He now works some 70 hours a week keeping up with orders.

An armoire in dyed pine and basswood (shown in the photo below) began with a pair of doors he had originally made for his sister. Wiley installed them in a shop she owned, but when the business faltered, the doors became the foundation for this piece of furniture. Wiley's design borrows from Russian motifs and the work of Nicolai Fechin. Fechin influences also are at work in the wall-hung mirror carved in pine that he made for an aunt (shown in the photo above right).

WILEY'
his nee
expand
der roo

WILEY
model
design
make

European designs. He was intrigued by the work of Russian-born artist Nicolai Fechin, who moved to Taos in 1927. As his skill developed, Wiley backtracked to learn more about traditional methods of furniture construction—he needed a context for the work. Wiley learned to blend his talents, creating casework and other pieces of furniture enlivened by chip-carved details and large relief-carved panels.

Wiley's output includes architectural millwork as well as furniture, so a midsize table saw and a large miter saw are central to Wiley's extensive collection of power tools. "But what I really like are the hand tools," he says, "a sharp handsaw or a smoothing plane."

Even more important is his collection of Swiss, German, and Japanese carving tools arranged neatly in a rack behind his workbench. It is one of his favorite spots in the shop. He has dozens of carving tools. Although they look similar, Wiley says the tools all have their own personalities. His favorite is the German Dastra.

AN OUTDOOR STRUCTURE Wiley built of railfoad ties and peeled logs offers protection from New Mexico's intense sunlight, allowing him to work outside.

Solitude as Muse

Wiley's shop has come together slowly, and it has the inevitable air of a building that has long outgrown its original purpose. Yet Wiley has few complaints. If he had the chance, he would replace his old Ashley wood-burning stove with radiant-floor heat. And he might opt for a slightly higher roof. Otherwise, Wiley finds that his "cobbled together" shop suits him.

And so does his community. Taos is a busy tourist town just up the road, its streets lined with galleries and restaurants. It has become something of a mecca for artists. Although Wiley is in Taos often, he and his wife live in Los Cordovas, a settlement of about 25 families three miles south of Taos.

Their property is bordered by a small river. It's quiet there, with only one other business in town. Wiley appreciates the solitude his property and workshop afford, finding them an ideal environment for incubating new carving and furniture designs away from the clatter of a busy town. When he needs a break from work, he just steps out the back door of his shop and spends time in the garden.

WILEY'S FIRST woodworking job was installing trim in his sister's house, but he quickly discovered a love for carving furniture details, like the rope pattern along the edge of this chair seat.

"Basically, we do just about anything in the shop that can't be done in the farmhouse or a cold barn."

A Shop Run Wild

WOOD PEGS and simple brackets hold a variety of tools within easy reach. The electrically powered whetstone at center sharpens tools without burning the steel.

THE HILLTOP SETTING for William Turner's shop in Maine is one the state's tourism office would happily package for resale if only it could. There is the distant view of Penobscot Bay and an occasional lobster boat, the sound of the wind ruffling the thick spruce forest, and the calls of gulls, ravens, and crows. His house is 700 ft. away, down a road that is sometimes passable in winter only with the help of steel crampons strapped to his boots. Turner has resorted to makeshift sleds to cart finished work away. There are no other buildings in sight.

139

"My shop and work aren't the center of my life. They are part of my identity as an individual, but they don't all-consume me."

KEEPING UP with demand has taught Stinson to work quickly. He can turn up to 30 green bowls in a single day.

A Turner's Life

THERE IS NOTHING architecturally graceful about Don Stinson's shop. It is a one-story, no-nonsense metal building with a concrete slab, paneled in plywood and illuminated by rows of bare light bulbs. Its ceiling is covered with clear polyethylene. Everything about the 1,500-sq.-ft. structure speaks to Stinson's devotion to production turning: the piles of logs outside the door waiting to be chunked into bowl-size bites, the manure conveyor he has adapted to move the piles of wood shavings, and the heap of rough burls that

Abrams has made banjos, guitars, dulcimers, harps, and tracker organs over the course of his career and now concentrates on an instrument called the octave mandolin.

A Shop in Concert

ABRAMS GOT LUCKY when a friend phoned to offer him a surplus workbench from a St. Louis trade school that was dropping its pattern-making classes. Made in the early 1900s, the bench included a swiveling pattern-maker's vise.

I F IT WEREN'T FOR AN OLD BANJO, Robert Abrams's life might have taken a completely different direction. Abrams picked up the instrument not long after he got out of high school. Already a musician, Abrams wanted to play the banjo, but it needed repairs and he had no idea where to start. He was introduced to Edward Fuchs, whose day job was restocking shotguns for Browning but whose real interest was in making instruments.

Abrams bugged him with so many questions that Fuchs finally offered him a job. His two-year stint with

BUILDING REGULATIONS in Portsmouth, New Hampshire, did not permit instrument maker Robert Abrams to have a detached workshop, so he added a second floor to an existing one-car garage. A gable vent that was no longer needed became the outline of a painted trillium, the icon Abrams picked for his line of mandolins.

Fuchs in St. Louis was the first of many jobs that allowed Abrams to intertwine a life of music with that of craftsmanship. He has made banjos, guitars, dulcimers, harps, and tracker organs over the course of his career and now concentrates on an instrument called the octave mandolin. It is a graceful, rounded eight- or ten-string instrument with a bigger sound than a standard mandolin. All the while he has been a musician as well, playing in nightclubs and coffee houses, at cider pressings, and square dances.

Working at Home

Abrams's one-man company, Trillium Octave Mandolins, is located in what had been a garage attached to his house. Abrams had considered building a separate shop, but zoning regulations in Portsmouth did not permit one in the quiet residential neighborhood where he lives. So several years ago, Abrams hired a builder who helped him

ALTHOUGH ABRAMS specializes in octave mandolins (the instrument in the center), he both makes and plays a variety of other musical instruments.

MANDOLINS AND a guitar body hang in a second-floor finishing area where they will get multiple coats of water-based lacquer. After experimenting with newer finishes for years, Abrams eventually made the switch from traditional nitrocellulose lacquer.

transform the one-car garage into a comfortable, efficient work space and allowed Abrams to escape his cramped basement workshop.

The builder neatly sliced the roof from the top of the 16-ft. by 24-ft. garage, raised the roof with four hydraulic bottle jacks and then built new 6-ft.-high walls to support it. The result is 768 sq. ft. on two floors: a main workroom below and a storage and a finishing room above. "It's very comfortable for making small things," says Abrams amid a collection of power tools neatly arranged around him. Big pieces of furniture would be more of a problem.

Radiant-floor heat—a network of hot-water tubing installed be- neath the floor—keeps Abrams comfortable without requiring hot-air vents or radiators. A separate circuit takes care of the second floor. Abrams works through frigid New Hampshire winters in a T-shirt with

For Loran Smith, installing a plywood wall festooned with plastic climbing grips was the natural outgrowth of a rock-climbing passion.

High Flyer

SMITH WORKS while his daughter, Meaghan, practices on a climbing wall. The plywood structure, peppered with holes to allow climbing holds to be repositioned, extends from the shop floor to the peak of the shop addition. They use only the first 11 ft.

PLENTY OF WOODWORKERS hang dart boards on their shop walls, but few blow off steam during the day by jumping on a 20-ft. climbing wall that runs from the shop floor to the peak of a second-floor wood loft. For Loran Smith, installing a plywood wall festooned with plastic climbing grips was the natural outgrowth of a rock-climbing passion so intense that it steered him away from an office job.

When he left college and began to look for work, he was disappointed to discover prospective employers expected

LORAN SMITH describes his New Hampshire home and shop as "a New Englander that follows the classic big house, little house, back house, barn" pattern. What had been a garage at the back of the house became his original shop, expanded a few years later with a two-story wing.

IN THIS UTILITARIAN TOOL CABINET, drawer bottoms are nailed directly to the bottom of the drawer boxes with sides overhanging enough to fit in grooves in the cabinet sides. It holds a collection of Stanley Bailey planes. The only one missing is a No. 1, but Smith's favorite is the No. 6 given to him by his wife's godfather.

a nine-to-five schedule, maybe even work on Saturdays. That's not what he had in mind. Smith wanted to spend more time climbing, so he took a job with a friend in construction who allowed him to come and go as he wanted. "I could show up and say, 'I'm leaving for Yosemite for two months,' and he'd say, 'See you when you get back.'"

A Start in Finish Carpentry

The arrangement with his buddy had proved ideal. Smith worked for the small construction company for several years and then went to a larger company, where he eventually supervised a 17-person finish-carpentry crew. He later went out on his own, and at first, he did everything from painting to building additions. Gradually his interests turned to kitchens and high-end finish work and finally to furniture.

Largely self-taught, Smith read everything he could get his hands on. He attended meetings of the Guild of New Hampshire Woodworkers, then went home to practice what he had seen. He recalls attending one Saturday meeting and seeing David Lamb carve a claw-and-ball foot. He spent all Sunday trying one and took it to the next meeting for a critique. Lamb suggested more practice. By the time the first job requiring such a foot came along a few years later, Smith was confident he could handle it.

Garage Conversion

Smith and his wife bought a house 10 years ago that followed the classic New England blueprint of a main house with additions built as they were needed. For several years, he worked in what had been a garage attached to the back of the house. Smith installed wiring and dust collection beneath the floor, insulated the walls, and hung drywall between exposed timbers.

When he needed more room, he added an 18-ft. by 28-ft. two-story wing. His old shop became his bench and assembly room, where he spends most of his time. The new wing, complete with climbing wall, is his machine room.

A STAIR FIT FOR A CLIMBER

Loran Smith planned his shop by arranging scaled templates of tools, benches, and other objects on a drawing of the building's footprint. He had trouble, however, giving up the room that would be required to build a conventional stairway to a second-floor wood-storage loft. His answer was a combination ladder and stair.

When not in use, the stair is held against the wall by a simple wood turn button (see photo at left). When Smith needs to get some lumber, he leans it against a header between two rafters (see photo at right). Rising at an angle of about 70 degrees, the stairway is much steeper than usual but its 5½-in.-wide treads provide plenty of footing for a mountain climber. A chin-up bar attached to the back helps keep Smith in top shape for his rock-climbing passion.

Smith has ample wood storage above both parts of the shop. After repeatedly banging his head on heating ducts in his first shop—the basement of an apartment where they lived—he also gave the new shop a 10-ft. ceiling.

Classic Designs

Although he started by making Shaker furniture, Smith now makes mostly Early American furniture designs. He takes occasional millwork jobs in addition to furniture commissions, so his work schedule is varied. One special job was making a Dunlap-style bookcase on desk in tiger maple for U.S. Sen. Judd Gregg of New Hampshire.

Although Smith works a solid 40-hour week in the shop, he still reserves time for community volunteer work and family vacations. Trips often include climbing. His daughter, Meaghan, is herself a serious climber, who is good enough to compete nationally. Smith's climbing wall, in fact, was installed mainly for the benefit of his daughter's training. At age ten, he says, she was climbing as well as he did when he was 19.

THIS FEDERAL-STYLE table was Smith's first veneered piece after attending a Guild meeting and buying a homemade vacuum-bag press for $100. Aprons are crotch mahogany and makore; the central medallion is curly birch. At the top of the legs are inlays of birch burl that Smith saved from a pile of firewood.

"I like the feel of space. It probably affects my work in some way I don't understand."

Master of Curves

A LARGE ROOF TRUSS speaks to the three years that Osgood spent studying architecture. He found he preferred the scale of furniture, in part because he could exert more control over it than he could on larger structures. The low-ceilinged area, a converted family room/kitchen, marks Osgood's first shop in the house.

ANYONE FAMILIAR WITH THE WORK of Jere Osgood would enter his rural New Hampshire workshop fully expecting to see something unusual, even wonderful. The shop itself is well equipped and spacious, but it is Osgood's command of tools and a subtly of design that steals the show. On this particular day, Osgood is working on three pieces of furniture, all of which show his trademark disdain for flat surfaces and straight lines.

A WALL OF sloping, south-facing windows in the New Hampshire workshop of Jere Osgood helps gather heat during the winter and provides ample natural light all year round. Osgood bought the house in the early 1980s and immediately transformed a combined family room and kitchen into a shop. He expanded a few years later.

One bench holds two semicircular scalloped hoods in ebony veneer that look something like two giant clam shells. They are the mating halves to a desk that's in for refinishing and then on its way to a new owner. Next to it is a low bench in beech, which Osgood's shop assistant, Nicola Cadrain, is going over carefully with sandpaper. At the far end of the room is a walnut sideboard, whose sides and front surfaces flow gently from one compound curve to another. Fitting the curved doors and drawer fronts in that piece would be especially difficult, but nothing is out of line, and reveals around doors and drawers are all exactly the same. It is typically Osgood: curving surfaces that flow precisely and seamlessly together. Cadrain, who has worked with Osgood for nearly 15 years, looks at the sideboard and asks, "It looks alive, like it's breathing, doesn't it?"

Family Room Turned Shop

Osgood has been in this shop for about 20 years, ever since he moved up from Boston and bought a house near the schools his two sons attended. A combined family room and kitchen, with a ceiling of just over 7 ft., was the unlikely beginning of a shop that now totals about 1,600 sq. ft.

He punched out one wall and added a room dominated by a three-story bank of south-facing windows, which flood the space with

WITH THE PEAK of the roof some 18 ft. off the floor and lights mounted well beyond the reach of errant lumber, the main floor of Osgood's shop seems spacious and open despite the fact that it's full of equipment and benches. To the right of the small drafting table is a set of stairs leading to wood storage below the main floor.

A WALL-MOUNTED tool chest, along with
secondhand storage drawers below, may be
the only rectilinear furniture to be found in
Osgood's shop. He doesn't like straight lines
and often finds it difficult to leave any surface
completely flat.

natural light. Here Osgood keeps his bench, a big drawing table, and
a few pieces of woodworking equipment. All electric lighting is
incandescent—Osgood hates fluorescent lights—with the bottom
edge of the reflectors set 11 ft. off the floor so they won't get bumped
by long pieces of lumber. The peak of the roof is 18 ft. high.

"I like the feel of space," Osgood says. "It probably affects my
work in some way I don't understand." Down a set of stairs, below
the window wall, sits a wood-storage area jammed with lumber and
veneer. At one end, shelves and compartments hold short lengths of
wood that Osgood couldn't bring himself to throw away. He jokes that

when he gets too old to heft heavy pieces of lumber he'll have an ample supply of shorts already on hand.

Dump the Pool, Too

In the mid-1980s, Osgood added another room, this one 16 ft. wide and 45 ft. long, where an aboveground swimming pool once stood. Former owners reached the pool by going out a pair of sliding doors from the family room/kitchen that Osgood had already turned into shop space. Without one, Osgood certainly didn't need the other. "It was all very cozy," he says, "but I didn't want it."

The new addition houses lumber and tools and provides a space to assemble furniture. Cadrain keeps her bench at one end of the room and beyond is additional wood storage and a spray booth. There is a second bench near the bandsaw, where a second helper or apprentice can work. No space has been wasted.

NICOLA CADRAIN, Osgood's assistant of 15 years, works on a set of four joined legs. Although Osgood handles design and joinery himself, he is appreciative of Cadrain's sensitivity in giving furniture its subtle contours and shapes. On her own time, Cadrain is a carver.

MAKING TAPERED LAMINATIONS

If Jere Osgood can find a way to take a flat surface and turn it into a contour, he's likely to jump at the chance. His furniture, in fact, often seems composed of interlocking curves and contours with a minimum of straight lines and right angles.

Although curved parts can be cut from solid material, it is often more practical to make them from thin layers of wood that are bent around a solid form. What results is called a bent lamination. It is not only stronger than a sawn member, but it also shows uniform grain and figure. Moreover, bent laminations produce less waste.

A simple bent lamination—one of uniform thickness—can be tapered in width, but cutting it so it tapers in thickness reveals unattractive gluelines and makes it weaker. Tapering the individual plies in a thickness planer before the lamination is glued together solves the problem. The lamination that results can be thinner at one end than the other, with no gluelines and no loss of strength.

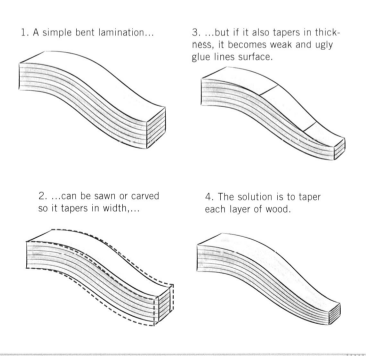

1. A simple bent lamination...

2. ...can be sawn or carved so it tapers in width,...

3. ...but if it also tapers in thickness, it becomes weak and ugly glue lines surface.

4. The solution is to taper each layer of wood.

OSGOOD PURCHASED this Amstrup horizontal mortising machine in Denmark after studying there in 1961. This three-phase machine is typical of the heavy, precise equipment that Osgood favors. He has owned some secondhand machines for 40 years.

Jigs and templates hang from walls and are stacked on spare bench space. Some of Osgood's smaller machines are mounted on wheels so they can be moved around. Lumber racks, made from angle iron painted a festive yellow, run floor to ceiling and use up wall space that would otherwise be wasted.

Rooms are finished simply with pine boards and no fussy details: A window to the immediate left of Osgood's wall-mounted tool case never even got any casing. Osgood says he's been picking away at the building ever since he bought it, but it is clear he'd rather be making furniture.

Tools Fit for the Task

Osgood has owned much of his equipment for a long time. Some of it dates from the early 1960s, and a few tools were used when he bought them. They are solid and heavy, chosen for their capacity to do precise work: a 27-in. Northfield bandsaw, a Hoffmann planer-jointer with a four-knife head that can plane highly figured stock into thin pieces without tearing it apart, and a squat Danish-made horizontal mortiser. "You just have to invest in really good machines," Osgood says as he looks at the giant bandsaw. "It costs as much as a car, I guess."

There is also the Polish-made shaper running on three-phase power, which is so heavy that Osgood installed posts beneath the floor to support it. Just as important are Osgood's drawing implements. He allows ideas for new furniture to percolate until he's comfortable with them and then works out the details in full-scale drawings. He keeps a small drafting table beneath the wall of windows, but there is also a much larger work surface nearby for big drawings.

Heavy, high-quality tools are essential for Osgood's work. He uses a wide range of solid woods and veneers in his work, and joinery and construction tend to be complicated. Without machines that can be set precisely, the work would be doubly difficult.

As capable as all the equipment might be, none of it would amount to a thing if weren't for Osgood's sense of design, his willingness to experiment, and his masterful use of the material. And Osgood has been unusually productive in this shop. In addition to smaller pieces, Osgood makes two major pieces a year, and his furniture can be found in a number of permanent collections, including the Museum of Fine Arts in Boston, the American Craft Museum in New York, and the Renwick Gallery in Washington, D.C. He has written and taught widely and in 2002 was awarded, along with British masters Alan Peters and John Makepeace, a lifetime achievement award by The Furniture Society.

Osgood, now in his late 60s, has cut his teaching schedule and might be expected to ease up in other ways. But in watching Osgood move about his shop, it is hard to imagine him changing stride. In accepting his Furniture Society award, he indicated that slowing down is not at all what he has in mind. "I feel that I am at a corner now in my career," he said. He has been working on a completely new process of lamination that will allow him to push ahead with new furniture designs. So much for retirement.

TYPICAL OF Osgood's love of curved lines, a table uses twin legs at each corner. Contours and compound curves enliven Osgood's furniture but sharply increase its complexity and difficulty of construction. Among his many accolades is a Lifetime Achievement Award given by the Furniture Society last year.

Like Rolland's path to
furniture making, his
shop is not entirely
conventional.

Earth-Berm Shop

ROLLAND ADOPTED innova-
tive construction methods in
building his earth-bermed
New Mexico workshop. Where
a finished exterior wall was
needed, he used stucco over
expanded metal lath. The
metal duct to the right of the
door is for a dust collector he
keeps outside; the PVC pipe
next to it is a conduit for an
air-compressor line.

A FTER WORKING IN THE 1980s at two New
England boatyards and as the first mate on the
schooners *Lewis French* and *American Eagle*,
Seth Rolland appeared headed for a life as a boatbuilder,
if not a blue-water sailor. But a six-month apprenticeship
with a New York custom furniture maker and then a
trip west pointed him in another direction.

By 1990, Rolland found himself in the high desert near
Taos, New Mexico. Next to the house that his future wife
was building, Rolland soon went to work on a workshop.

WHEN IT CAME TIME to add on, Rolland opted for a wood-truss roof, a dry-wall interior, and real glass panels instead of fiberglass. The floor is adobe hardened with boiled linseed oil.

A FLAT ROOF on the shop of furniture maker Seth Rolland collects rainwater, which can be used for irrigating trees in New Mexico's dry climate. The low wall to the right of the workshop is made from mortar and empty soda cans, providing an effective barrier with a minimum of materials.

USED TIRES packed with earth are a basic building block for walls in Rolland's shop. Expanded metal lath screwed to the tires provides a base for stucco. This wall separates the original shop from the later addition.

Like Rolland's path to furniture making, his shop is not entirely conventional. Much of it, for example, is below grade. And although the 1,100-sq.-ft. structure looks nothing like the clapboarded sheds, barns, and workshops of Rolland's New England past, it is well suited to an environment of intense sunlight, little rainfall, and temperature swings that reach 90°F in summer and 0°F degrees in winter.

An Inexpensive Solar Design

Rolland and his wife, Me'l Christensen, started small. Their first workshop was a 400-sq.-ft. solar design based on a plan by Mike Reynolds, a local architect. The approach was similar to the one Christensen had taken with her house. First came a 5-ft. deep hole carved in the ground by a backhoe. To form walls, the couple stacked used tires like bricks, ramming each course full of earth before laying the next. At the top of their tire wall, a 2x12 bond beam carries the Engleman spruce rafters that Rolland and Christensen peeled with draw knives.

Decking, insulation, and roofing followed. The entire south wall of the workshop is made of

THE ROOF IN Rolland's original shop is made of spruce logs that he and his wife peeled with drawknives. Beneath a skylight is some of Rolland's furniture, which he has shown at a number of galleries and juried exhibits.

TRANSLUCENT FIBERGLASS panels in Rolland's original 400-sq.-ft. workshop provide heat as well as light. Through the doorway is the larger addition he added several years later. Skylights help to cool the shop in summer.

translucent fiberglass panels, through which the sun provides the shop's only source of heat. A floor made of adobe—a mix of earth, sand, and straw—and hardened with linseed oil has proved roughly as hard as pine. It is easy on tools that are dropped, Rolland says, but durable. The couple worked in the mornings for a month to put the structure up and spent $2,500—about $6 a sq. ft.

Adding On

When it came time for a 700-sq.-ft. addition six years later, Rolland took a different approach. He called on friends and hired some help, while his wife spent the two-month construction period on a tour of Tibet. Like the original structure, the addition has an adobe floor, but Rolland used roof trusses instead of peeled spruce logs, spent more time on finishing touches, and used glass instead of fiberglass panels.

Skylights help to ventilate the workshop in summer, and windows admit sunlight for warmth in winter. Even without a conventional heating system, Rolland finds the shop comfortable most of the time.

RECIPE FOR AN ADOBE FLOOR

Seth Rolland's slab floor is easier on both his tools and his feet than concrete and is about as resilient underfoot as wood. But it is made from local materials that cost next to nothing: adobe, which is basically clay-rich earth that can be scooped from the building site, plus straw and sand. Finished with boiled linseed oil, the floor continues to harden for months after it is fabricated. Here's how to do it:

1. After leveling the excavated floor with a pick, combine one part adobe, one part sand, and a few handfuls of straw in a cement mixer with enough water to make a stiff mix. This is the scratch coat.

2. Trowel the mixture on the floor to a depth of 2 in. and scratch the surface to provide a mechanical bond with the next coat. Allow the scratch coat to cure for a week.

3. Mix a final coat of one part adobe, two parts sand, and a few handfuls of straw, combining them as before in a cement mixer. Trowel the mix-ture over the floor, smooth, and allow to cure for four days to five days. Then apply three coats of linseed oil, allowing the floor to dry between coats.

The result is a durable floor that is easy to repair. For the first six months of Rolland's floor, dropping a hammer on the floor would result in a dent, but the floor hardened enough over time to resist damage. Rolland repaired any gouges with excess epoxy left over during furniture glue-ups.

In the dead of winter, early-morning temperatures in the shop may hover in the 50s, but the room quickly warms as the sun rises.

Rolland kept costs down by using inexpensive or readily available materials—including aluminum soda cans for an exterior wall—and by skipping unnecessary frills. Expanded metal lath screwed to walls of stacked tires provides a solid foundation for stucco where exterior walls are exposed. One of the advantages of having a shop built mostly into the ground is that there is virtually no exterior finish.

Interior walls are built directly against excavated earth. They are gypsum drywall over a 2x4 frame, protected from water damage by a layer of plastic and the region's arid climate. Low tech and inexpensive, the buildings also went up quickly.

A Nontraditional Approach

If Rolland's New Mexico shop looks nontraditional, so does his furniture. There are no Shaker designs and no Early American reproductions. Producing both one-off and repeated designs, Rolland's work includes chairs, tables, entertainment centers, armoires, beds, and chests. He likes organic shapes, meaning lots of curves, and as a result often turns to bent laminations or steam bending to form furniture parts. His "Trimerous Chair," for example, is composed of a one-piece bent-laminated seat and back, tusklike front legs in curly maple, and arm assemblies in walnut that swoop downward to form the rear legs.

The curving legs on "Janna's Dining Table," in cherry and milk paint, look something like the muscular forelegs of an animal. His work has been featured in a number of regional shows and was the topic of a *Modern Master* segment on Home & Garden Television.

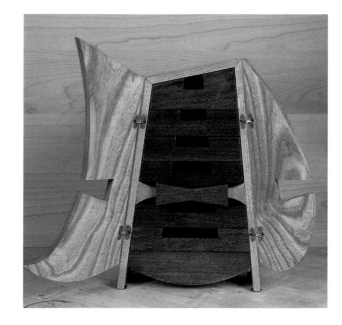

ROLLAND MADE this jewelry chest 10 years ago as he looked for ways to break away from rectilinear furniture forms. The ash and padauk piece was a trial run for an armoire.

"ASH EXPLOSION NO. 2" is a combination of glass, sandstone, ash, cherry, and basswood. Rolland sliced a 4-in. by 6-in. plank of ash to form 1-in.-sq. sections, then steam-bent the piece to allow insertion of cherry and basswood dividers. The ash is still connected at the far end.

"If the client wants input then I send them politely to another workshop."

Reviving an Ontario Homestead

SEPARATE BENCH and machine rooms help organize workflow in Michael Fortune's 3,400-sq.-ft. shop. At left is an unusual pneumatic work stand Fortune salvaged from an old upholstery warehouse. It grips a #1 chair, a design Fortune has made since 1979.

IT IS HARD TO IGNORE 18 tons of woodworking equipment spread over 3,400 sq. ft. of shop floor, but the most important part of Michael Fortune's studio is probably the modest design office at the northeast corner of the building. For 20 hours a week—on top of the 45 hours he spends on the shop floor—the celebrated Canadian furniture designer and maker wheels his chair to the drafting table and, with a fresh 6B pencil, puts ideas to paper. Through a window to his right he can see a massive veneer guillotine, a hydraulic press, a 14-in. table saw,

HIGH STANDARDS of craftsmanship, as well as innovative furniture designs, have won Fortune wide professional recognition and a long list of loyal clients. Some order pieces over a period of many years.

and other equipment with industrial-size appetites. But it is Fortune's creative push that has given these tools their unique usefulness and purpose.

A Start in Graphic Arts

Working exclusively to his own designs, Fortune and two assistants make furniture for public and private clients in Canada, the United States, and beyond. Affable and unpretentious, Fortune still does not bend easily on design. "If the client wants input," he says, "then I send them politely to another workshop." His clients are content to play by his rules. Some of them order furniture over and over again, collecting as many as a dozen and a half pieces in a 10- or 20-year span. His work is as technically precise at it is innovative, sometimes incorporating metal as well as solid wood and veneers in gracefully contoured shapes.

As widely known as Fortune has become, he backed into his trade. He originally enrolled as a graphic arts student at the Sheridan College School of Craft and Design. He switched to furniture design after wandering by mistake into the college's woodworking shop in 1971, where he was unable to resist the sales pitch of Don McKinley, the man running the program. After graduation, Fortune worked as an intern for several months with Alan Peters, the English furniture maker. Soon he was working on his own designs.

Fortune calls his approach evolutionary, working on a single idea over a length of time until "it eventually evolves into something new." There were some difficult years, but in 1980, a Toronto couple bought a dining table and eight chairs, and now there are no idle moments in Fortune's shop. Fortune has since been inducted into the Royal Canadian Academy of Arts, and in 1993 was awarded the Prix Saidye Bronfman Award, Canada's foremost prize for excellence in craft. He is a frequent teacher at workshops and an adviser to other woodworkers.

Escape from the City

Until only a few years ago, Fortune worked in rented spaces in Toronto. He and fellow artists would move into a relatively inexpensive part of town. Eventually, restaurants and shops followed until, inevitably, the area became trendy. When that happened, rents would go up. It seemed a frustrating cycle, but Fortune was working on an alternative.

Through a quirk in Canadian law, he had 20 years earlier been able to buy for $1 (Canadian) an 1831 homestead in the Kawartha Lakes region to the east of Toronto. Part of the deal was that he repair the cabin, which is one of the oldest surviving homesteads in the province. The roof had caved in. There were no windows. Grass grew in what became their living room.

Tackling one major project a year, Fortune and his family gradually turned the dilapidated cedar log cabin into a restored family getaway. The property abuts Crown land—the Canadian equivalent of a national park—and it provided enough space for Fortune to build a shop some 400 ft. from the cabin.

His shop was constructed in two stages, the first 2,200-sq.-ft. structure in 1998 and then another 1,200 sq. ft. was added two years later.

ONCE FORTUNE moved his woodworking operation from a shop in downtown Toronto to a country setting, he found a hidden advantage: Ground-floor windows could be installed without fear of compromising security.

FORTUNE FAVORS old woodworking equipment. Two hydraulic pistons that sit atop this 1930s' veneer guillotine force down a bar that immobilizes veneer so it can be sliced with a 7-ft.-long knife. The cuts made on 2-in.-thick stacks of veneer are as precise as those on a single thickness of wood.

The T-shaped building has separate machine and bench rooms. It is well insulated against Ontario's frigid winters and has a 14-ft. ceiling and lots of windows. "It's quite wonderful," he says. "I don't get caught in traffic and the rest of it. In a lot of ways, it's an ideal environment."

Rescuing Old Iron

Fortune has found a complementary calling in nurturing old woodworking machinery back to health. Every piece of equipment in his shop was bought used—some of the machines are now robust septuagenarians—for a few hundred dollars a shot. He can strip down an old machine, remake broken or worn parts, and put it back in service in better-than-new condition.

His studio collection bears him out. It includes a slot mortiser that was used to make M-1 carbides during World War II, a planer and jointer picked up from a high-school shop program that was closing its doors, and the 1930s' Ruckle veneer guillotine that reduces what would be an afternoon's work of cutting veneer by hand to only a few minutes.

Although he has three bandsaws, he is still using a 15-in. General that was one of the first tools he acquired. It has its original tires and guide blocks, and Fortune adds, "It's a peach." When he needs to add to a tool, Fortune taps into a network of dealers and like-minded tool aficionados who keep their eyes open until they find what he's looking for. The process can take months.

Fortune's bond with tools and what they can accomplish has been a long time in the making. An uncle began buying tools for Fortune when he was eight years old: a Stanley block plane, a framing square, a bench grinder, a vise. At 12, Fortune was given a table saw for Christmas and promptly began work on a kayak from plans he ordered from *Popular Mechanics*. He learned early that making birdhouses and lawn furniture produced pocket money.

An Orderly Environment

Fortune finds both safety and order important attributes of a successful studio, believing that a workmanlike attitude is as essential as imaginative designs and impeccable craftsmanship. As busy as his

FORTUNE FINDS a workmanlike attitude is a key part of running a successful furniture studio, and that means keeping tools in good repair and his work area organized. Jigs for this drill press hang nearby where they are easily accessible.

FORTUNE'S 1950S' Hubert hydraulic veneer press can be set up to use its three platens in tandem or separately, depending on the job. In the foreground is an early thickness sander made in Italy.

ECLECTIC STYLE

The celebrated work of Michael Fortune draws on a number of furniture styles and traditions, from Charles Rennie Mackintosh to Frank Lloyd Wright and Hans Wegner. An extensive collection of woodworking equipment, in addition to well-honed design and construction skills, allows Fortune to execute complex plans with authority and grace. His work is found in a number of public and private collections.

A music stand (facing page) from 1990 combines curly maple and Macassar ebony. The top is vacuum formed. A pair of chairs, called "No. 1 Revisited," dating from about the same time, are cast aluminum and vacuum-formed lacewood veneer (below). His demilune cabinet, made of Macassar ebony with an interior of curly cherry, was made to hold the best of a client's massive record collection (right). Fortune built the cabinet in 2002.

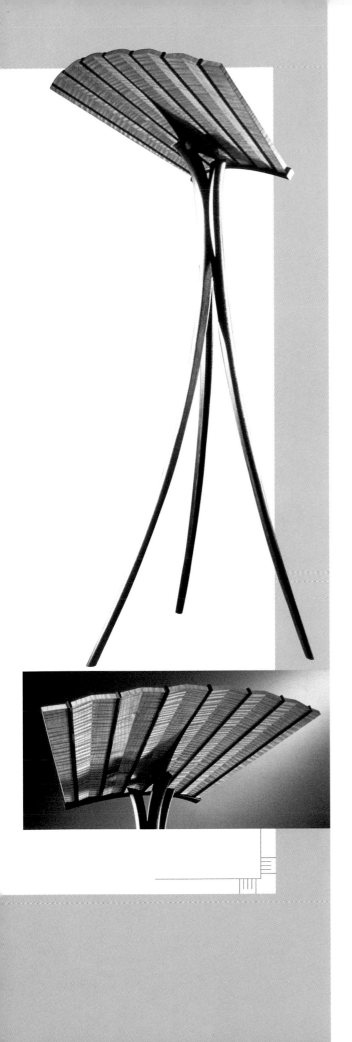

JEFF WHALEN, Fortune's
lead assistant, works on a
furniture commission—one
of several typically underway
in Fortune's studio at any
given time. Attention to
safety equipment and safe
practices—safety glasses,
ear protection, and efficient
dust removal—has helped
prevent injuries to Fortune
and his employees.

shop may be, he believes "absolutely nothing" is worth the risks inherent to working quickly or without adequate machine guards. It may be because of his approach that neither he nor any of his employees have ever had an accident on the job.

He likes the shop to be kept clean and the tools in good repair. In carefully orchestrating the many parts of his working environment, Fortune has kept in mind mentor Alan Peters's compound in the Devon countryside where shop and home are closely intertwined. After working there, he was impressed with how Peters exerted complete control over Peters's life. He worked directly with his clients, designed the furniture he wanted to make, and then made it in his shop. With both workshop and living quarters essentially under one roof, Peters experienced no uneven transitions between work and his life outside work. It was all there. Over time, Fortune has succeeded in creating the same environment. Work, family, and the outside world are all in balance.

Schmidt is an imaginative experimenter, but he also is a highly precise woodworker who can build complicated furniture designs to extremely tight tolerances.

High Precision, High Style

SCHMIDT CREATES precise scale drawings of furniture before he makes it, a skill taught at his alma mater, the North Bennet Street School in Boston. The gas-fired heater hanging from the ceiling above him heats his 2,500-sq.-ft. shop.

THE THREE-STORY BRICK BUILDING at 855 Islington Street, well off the Portsmouth waterfront, was originally a factory where mattress buttons were made. During World War II, it was a military barracks and, later, a gym. For years, though, it has just been called the Button Factory. It is the home of many artisans: a dozen woodworkers on the first floor alone, an organ builder, a handful of painters and photographers, jewelers, a luthier, and even a papermaker.

SCHMIDT (right) and shop mate David Leach work on a mahogany bench bound for a show in Paris.

They are all neighbors to Scott Schmidt, whose ground-level, two-room shop covers 2,500 sq. ft. It is high ceilinged and fragrant with wood dust, the concrete floor wearing through its layer of battleship-gray paint. Schmidt's rooms are crowded with racks of lumber, industrial-size woodworking equipment, furniture still under construction, and finished pieces either on the way out or arriving back at the shop after a show. A visitor might find him at a big drafting board at the end of the room, Charles Mingus playing softly on the shop's audio system.

PACKED WITH nearly 20 years of woodworking acquisitions, Scott Schmidt's shop relies heavily on an the 20-in., three-phase table saw made by the Northfield Foundry and Machine Company of Minnesota. When he calls the company for technical information, he finds himself talking with the grandson of the man who built it.

Inspiration in Unlikely Places

Like many graduates of the North Bennet Street School in Boston, Schmidt still makes precise drawings of all the pieces he builds. Yet his furniture looks nothing like the 18th-century American classics that North Bennet students typically build during their two years of study (see p. 56).

(see p. 56)

He looks for design ideas everywhere and sometimes finds them in unlikely places. One of his favorite objects is a carved 19th-century Maori war club made without benefit of metal tools. Schmidt thinks it comes from the Fiji Islands. An odd crook on the end of the club was designed to fit snugly in the hollow of a man's throat; with a twist of the club, the attacker dispatched the victim by breaking his neck. Despite its grim history, Schmidt finds the club beautifully made and superbly balanced, attributes he tries to build into the furniture he makes. He hefts the leg of a chair he's making, then the war club, as he compares their weight and balance. Never mind that as functional objects, they have no connection. Furniture making, he concedes, is a "private obsession."

Schmidt has picked up a variety of other design ideas from Pacific art objects. Others ideas are born on the spot. He recalls a visit to the home of some potential clients with tastes far more traditional than his own. They sat together in the living room and labored to find common ground for a commission Schmidt would undertake. Schmidt spotted a wooden box with an ovoid pattern embossed on one side, tucked on an upper shelf. The unusual pattern was the eye of a fish. He played with the shape in his mind and began exploring it with the clients. What resulted was a set of three nesting

A DESIGN FOR three nesting tables in wenge sprang from Schmidt's observation that the clients had an old wooden box high on a shelf with an ovoid shape—the eye of a salmon—embossed on the side.

tables with open, oval sides that look like the stylized fish-eye design on the side of the box. His clients never would have thought that's what they were after, but they love the tables.

Experimental Materials

Schmidt has worked extensively with wenge, mainly because his customers keep asking for it. There are some woods he won't touch—ebony, for example, or rosewood—just because they have been harvested so mercilessly.

His interest in material goes far beyond planks of lumber. He worked for a year to perfect a tabletop material cast from wood, metal dust, and epoxy resin. New experiments are aimed at perfecting a similar material made from a mix of green coffee beans and resin. The

MAKING TEMPLATES

Templates help guide machines in quickly producing a number of duplicate parts. Bearing-guided bits on a router table or shaper follow the contours of the template so that the shape has to be produced only once. Scott Schmidt's approach is to start with plywood that's ¼ in. thick. It can be cut and shaped by hand with ease.

When he's satisfied with the shape, Schmidt screws the plywood to a thicker and more durable piece of material—here it's ¾-in. medium-density fiberboard—and produces a finished template on a shaper. What results is a durable template that can be used to run off many identical parts.

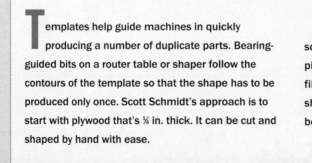

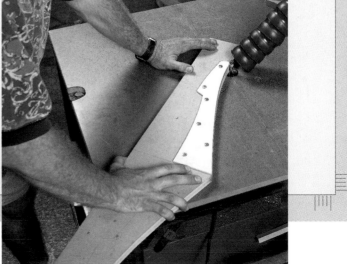

composite is rock hard but develops an interesting texture.

Schmidt is an imaginative experimenter with materials, shapes, and textures, but he also is a highly precise woodworker who can build complicated furniture designs to extremely tight tolerances. Complex curves and tapers, which must be duplicated in batch runs, are routine. He has worked out a system of making templates that helps.

SHAPER KNIVES, some of them custom ground, are essential for making complex parts in much of Schmidt's furniture. He says a serious accident on his shaper a decade ago was a classic case of distraction: pushing too hard on a Friday afternoon, a newly born daughter at home, Christmas right around the corner.

Tools with a History

Schmidt has had 18 years in his shop to build a sizable collection of vintage woodworking equipment. One of the first pieces was a 12-in. patternmaker's jointer, a $4,000 piece of heavy-duty equipment made in 1959 by Northfield. He sold a piece of furniture he'd made at North Bennet Street so he could afford to buy it. He has a 16-in. radial-arm saw, also made by Northfield, which dates from 1949, and a 20-in. Northfield table saw; it's only 30 years old.

There is a smattering of modern equipment as well, including a milling and drilling machine with three-way adjustments that will handle either wood or metal—and the shaper that nearly cost him his left hand 10 years ago. Rushing to finish a job on a Friday afternoon, Schmidt was pushing the last of many chair parts over a bit that cut a deep cove profile. His hand was pulled into the machine, severing one finger and mangling two others. Under the gun to finish the project, Schmidt was back at work the following Monday. After half a dozen additional surgeries and painful physical therapy, he has regained most of the use of the fingers.

Schmidt's grandfather was a dentist, and one of his most prized tools is a dental chair that has been converted for use as a vise stand. Schmidt has at least two vise-equipped benches in the shop, but he brings his workpiece to the dental-chair stand when he wants to detail it by hand. The odd piece of equipment might look out of place in most shops. Yet here, where a Pacific Rim war club becomes an interpretative foundation for modern furniture, the chair-turned-vise fits right in.

A DENTIST'S CHAIR, stripped of its seat and equipped with a pair of vises, makes a sturdy and completely adjustable vise. Schmidt thinks the mechanism, still with a painted wood-grain design around the base, dates from the 1920s.

> Even though Cotter could not find the trained artisans he wanted, he coaxed the same results from a variety of sophisticated equipment.

COTTER'S FAVORITE TOOL is a CNC router, which can process as many as 10 sheets of plywood an hour and cut out plywood pieces for a full set of kitchen cabinets in a single day. Although the device speeds construction of basic cabinet boxes, doors and face frames are still made conventionally.

Machine Power

SOON AFTER MOVING FROM IRELAND to the eastern end of Long Island, New York, Stephen Cotter went to work as a trim carpenter. He began building cabinets on site, then moved into a cabinetmaking shop, where he worked for a builder. A few years later, at the urging of an architect he frequently worked with, Cotter launched his own cabinetmaking business. It was only then that he learned there was a downside to the very building boom that promised to bring him so much business.

COTTER'S SHOP is located in a mostly industrial area in Speonk near the eastern end of Long Island. At 4,500 sq. ft., the shop feels small even though the business has only three full-time workers .

COTTER'S WIFE, Kimberly, helps when the shop gets busy. Specialized computer software generates cutting lists for cabinet parts and then sends instructions to other equipment in the shop. A reliance on sophisticated tooling has allowed the shop to turn out big kitchens with a small staff.

Full of expectations, Cotter soon learned the surge of building projects in the region had already absorbed the skilled labor he needed for his own shop—at least a cabinetmaking shop in the traditional sense. How do you open a cabinet shop, he wondered, when there are no cabinetmakers to hire? Cotter was undaunted. He found that with sophisticated woodworking equipment, he could build the same cabinets with fewer of the trained artisans he once thought he'd need.

Booming Trade

Cotter started his business in a geographic area rich with potential. Communities like Westhampton and Southampton near Long Island's eastern tip are quintessentially upscale. Only a few hours from New York City, these towns provide summer and vacation retreats for the rich and famous, as well as an enviable market for a shop turning out good work. Even though Cotter could not find the trained artisans he wanted, he coaxed the same results from a variety of sophisticated equipment. Working mostly with architects and designers, Cotter now builds cabinetry for kitchens and libraries, entertainment centers, bathroom vanities, and other built-ins.

He works in a 4,500-sq.-ft. structure made from concrete block. Although the shop is large in comparison with most small cabinet shops, Cotter says one of his major needs is for more room and more electrical power. His shop is already packed. There is an immense Altendorf® sliding table saw, a computer-guided router, a wide-belt sander, a cutoff saw with a computer-guided fence, and an industrial-size jointer and shaper.

AN ALTENDORF table saw gives Cotter added production speed and precision and has helped offset a scarcity of skilled labor when he opened his shop in the mid-1990s. A large sliding table allows full sheets of plywood to be cut easily and with greater accuracy and safety, while a scoring blade eliminates chips in pricey surface veneers.

WORKING WITH computer-guided equipment has made Cotter's measuring tape optional. An automatic stop on his cutoff saw adjusts to dimensions that have either been entered on a keypad or pulled from computerized construction drawings. Just as important, settings don't wander: Cabinet parts cut to the same length on different days will be exactly the same length.

A New Way

Cotter has been dealing, of course, not only with a regional shortage of skilled labor but society's lowered interest in producing artisans skilled in manual trades. Traditional school shop programs haven't entirely disappeared, but there are fewer of them than there were a generation ago. Unlike Europe, the United States has no formal guild system that trains new generations of cabinetmakers and other artisans and then packs them off to rigorous apprenticeships. The trend is a source of common complaint among studio furniture makers.

Cotter found a way around the problem, however, and in the process discovered something interesting: He liked working the new way. His favorite tool is a Komo CNC (computer numerically controlled) router, a device driven by computer that takes the place of half a dozen workers and their machines. Sheet goods—cabinet plywood, for example, or medium-density fiberboard—remain stationary on the machine's bed while an overhead router guided by a computer program automatically makes the cuts. Unless Cotter has loaded the instructions incorrectly, there are no miscuts and no mistakes. The Komo can cut out the plywood parts for a complete set of kitchen cabinets, in perfect precision, in less than a day. "I have been able to make fun and tricky things with relative ease," Cotter says.

COTTER WOODWORKING turns out a variety of cabinets and built-ins, all of it custom ordered.

He works long hours—12 hours to 14 hours a day—and has only two full-time shop mates: an apprentice cabinetmaker and a finisher. His wife helps out when the shop gets busy. With machines doing a lot of the grunt work, Cotter splits his time between attending customer meetings, doing the shop drawings for upcoming jobs, and keeping an eye on what's going on in the shop.

Hand tools, the mainstay of most small cabinet shops, are few and far between. Cotter's arsenal amounts to a couple of block planes he uses chiefly when he's fine-tuning cabinets during an installation. Other than that, he simply doesn't need hand tools. He may not have foreseen this style of work when starting as a trim carpenter, but it has certainly had its rewards. "It's difficult to go back once you go forward."

> "I worked for a wood-
> worker years ago and
> his shop was very bad.
> I quit after a year,
> fearing for my health,
> swearing that my
> future shop would be
> the exact opposite."

A Dane in California

TWO PIVOTAL interests in Hjorth-Westh's life are the boat that carries him on summer fishing expeditions and the furniture he makes during the rest of the year. During the off season, the boat is stored in a shed attached to his shop.

E JLER HJORTH-WESTH'S WORKSHOP took shape slowly. Before handling a single piece of lumber, he and his wife, Karen, first had to clear their forested site a mile from the Pacific on California's North Coast. With an Alaska mill—a portable sawmill consisting of a powerful chainsaw and guide tracks—they cut structural timbers from the Douglas fir they had felled. Then they went to work.

It was slow going. Although Karen already had a house nearby, they were working without the convenience of

CALIFORNIA furniture maker Ejler Hjorth-Westh and his wife, Karen, began work on their wooded ridge-top lot in 1983, felling trees and working without electricity as they constructed a shop and, later, their house. Structural timbers were milled with a chainsaw.

IF HE HAD IT to do again, Hjorth-Westh would have built a stronger floor system and added more insulation, but overall his shop has been a success. A storeroom he added in 1999 doubled the shop's productivity.

electricity. They bought building materials when they could afford them, and they learned to work without power ("actually not a struggle," Hjorth-Westh says, "just a slow process"). The couple finally closed in the 1,600-sq.-ft. shop in 1986, more than two years after they started. Electricity came three years later. If it seems a steeper climb than most young furniture makers attempt, the process was perfectly in keeping with Hjorth-Westh's belief that hard work is an "essential calling."

From Boatbuilding to Furniture

The Danish-born Hjorth-Westh had worked as an apprentice in a boatyard on the coast north of San Francisco, and had originally planned to use the shop for building boats. He did, in fact, make himself a boat, a 19-ft. lap strake dory that he still uses for his annual summer fishing sabbaticals.

But in 1992, after attending the fine-furniture program at the nearby College of the Redwoods, Hjorth-Westh decided to switch to furniture making. He added insulation and lowered the ceiling in his shop to make a more practical work space, and in 1999 added a storeroom for wood, furniture, and his boat.

All of his work is built on commission. He makes dining sets, coffee tables, desks, chairs, and sideboards, most of it for clients who live within 25 miles of his shop. Curious about everything from politics to literature, Hjorth-Westh draws on new ideas for furniture wherever he can find them. "New clients provide a new set of parameters," he says, "and new inspiration. Also, the people I bring in to help with big jobs contribute. I am not a doctrinarian, and all ideas are weighed and tested."

Hjorth-Westh says his background in boatbuilding gave him "an obsession" for functionality, yet his furniture is anything but plain. Materials cover a wide swath: Swiss pear, bubinga, English cherry, ebony, wenge, madrone, and a variety of other hard- and softwoods. Furniture shapes are graceful and light.

A Shop of Curiosities

Hjorth-Westh's work space is not only a working studio but also something of a curiosity shop. There are, of course, the objects anyone would expect to find in a furniture maker's shop: his handmade wooden planes arranged neatly on wooden pegs, rows of bar clamps, and the collection of wood screws carefully stored in old pimento jars. But then there is the rest of it—a line of hats hanging from nails, a pair of small paper targets peppered with holes from a prized Spanish air pistol, photographs of the ocean where he fishes, and widgets and gizmos too numerous to catalog. "I also have a fairly impressive collection of animal skulls," Hjorth-Westh confides.

Hjorth-Westh is a self-described political junkie, and CNN is readily available. "I never know the day," he says, "but I know what time CNN is on." His television is perched on a bookshelf, and the books are not there for show. Hjorth-Westh can quote V. I. Lenin, Danish philosopher Søren Kierkegaard, and even Monty Python (his favorite: "We are all idiots").

Karen's professional catering skills also have a role to play. Her food is widely praised, so much so that Hjorth-Westh says it has become a draw for potential shop helpers. New visitors to the shop are shown around and then left to themselves while Ejler fetches scones or tea sandwiches Karen has made. "Some of my clients

CHAIRS NEARING completion are set aside in a storeroom next to Hjorth-Westh's shop. He upholsters them himself.

HJORTH-WESTH applies finish to a low table that reflects his taste for clean, uncluttered design.

HJORTH-WESTH, left, and apprentice German Plessl of Argentina work in a shop bearing evidence of diverse interests and a sense of exploration. Hjorth-Westh vowed after an early apprenticeship that his shop would be warm and comfortable.

HJORTH-WESTH'S wife, Karen, a professional caterer, supplies the food that has won over both shop helpers and potential clients. From left: apprentice German Plessl, Hjorth-Westh's niece Camilla and friend Michael visiting from Denmark, and the Hjorth-Wesths.

still speak of certain foods enjoyed at their first visit to my shop," he says. "Seduction with food is nothing new, and something both my wife and I understand very well."

Hjorth-Westh is reacting, at least in part, to less pleasant working environments he's experienced over the years. "I worked for a woodworker years ago and his shop was very bad—leaky roof, drafty, cold," Hjorth-Westh says. "The floor covered with debris and never swept. I quit after a year, fearing for my health, swearing that my future shop would be the exact opposite." By any measure, he has succeeded.

Not Hand Tools Alone

Hjorth-Westh's various apprenticeships, including his training with James Krenov, have fostered an appreciation for exacting work with hand tools. Still, the shop is well equipped with power tools, including a large Robland combination machine at the center of the room and a burly 1891 bandsaw.

A ceiling-mounted air cleaner reflects Hjorth-Westh's sometimes troublesome relationship with wood dust and a desire to keep his work space as clean as possible. Woods that were once harmless—wenge, for one—now bring on nettlesome rashes or allergies. "I see myself as being in a never-ending fight against noise and dust," he says. "I suspect allergies to be cumulative. Dust as a respiratory hazard also should be taken seriously as it has put many a woodworking career to a halt."

A Second Passion—Fishing

As comfortable as his shop may be, Hjorth-Westh willingly stops making furniture from August through October. He uses the time for chores neglected during the rest of the year, to gather firewood, to slim down, to enjoy the outdoors, and, most of all, to fish. He launches his dory from a nearby beach and goes for ling cod, a delicious although not altogether handsome fish. Compost derived from his catch helps to fertilize the couple's small vegetable garden.

But come October, it is time to light the woodstove and resume work inside, a process that rekindles familiar feelings and images for Hjorth-Westh: "the light from the weak sun, the cold moist air, the smells of fall, and that first fire beginning another year."

ALONG WITH the typical paraphernalia common to any woodworking shop, Hjorth-Westh's passions linger on the walls and shelves—target-practice paper for a beloved Spanish air pistol, photos of the ocean where he fishes, and a row of hats.

DOGHOLE DORY

Before converting his shop to furniture making, Ejler Hjorth-Westh had intended to build boats. *Valkyrie,* completed in 1987, was an admirable start. With a length overall of 19 ft., 11 in., and a beam of 56 in., the boat still weighs only 190 lb. It is made of ¼-in. mahogany plywood, white oak, madrone, mahogany, teak, and fir. It is a lap strake design, meaning that its hull is constructed by fastening overlapping strips of wood to an underlying frame.

Hjorth-Westh calls her a "doghole dory" after the term that early generations of coastal sailors called the small inlets dotting the northern California coast. A committed fisherman by summer, Hjorth-Westh designed his dory for beach launchings, more than 300 of them so far, and says she has helped him land some eight tons of fish since her original launch.

> There is more to it than a shop and a collection of tools. Martin has redirected his life, finding a deep satisfaction in the woods and hills around him.

Making a New Life

AFTER THE CANOE has been formed, it is finished with locally cut ash gunnels and custom hardwood decks. Martin switched from Western red cedar to white cedar cut nearby because of concerns about logging practices in the Pacific Northwest, as well as the long distances the lumber had to be trucked.

RANDY MARTIN'S WORK as a construction millwright, first as an apprentice and another eight years as a journeyman, took him to steel mills, chemical refineries, vinyl factories, and even nuclear power plants. He was a skilled metalworker whose assignments covered everything from moving a 20-ton press to prying the top off a blast furnace.

But in time, he grew disillusioned with heavy industry and the toll he was convinced it was taking on the environment. So he changed his life. With his partner, Dyan Jones, Martin moved to a small town some

A SPACIOUS main floor covering 880 sq. ft. is ample enough for Ontario woodworker Randy Martin to build and finish cedar-strip canoes. There are other benefits to plenty of open floor space: It gives Martin's band, Slipstream, a place to practice.

RATHER THAN BUY new building materials for a shop, Martin used a 19th-century timber frame that had originally been a house. Reassembled on his rural Ontario property, the frame became the skeleton of a spacious woodworking shop with 10-ft. ceilings on the first floor and a sizable storage loft above. Entry doors are also salvaged.

75 miles west of Toronto where he re-established himself as a country woodworker. He and Jones called their property Hawkwind. Martin's first task was to create a shop, and true to his conviction that natural resources should be used sparingly, he elected to recycle an old structure rather than construct a new one.

Recycling on a Grand Scale

Martin and Jones found a timber frame dating from the 1860s, which had originally been a Georgian-style house in Burlington, 60 miles to the southeast. He liked the idea of reusing it, so the couple trucked the frame to their property and rebuilt it, creating a shop 24 ft. wide and 40 ft. long. There is a full 10 ft. of headroom on the first floor and an 8-ft. ceiling upstairs.

Martin salvaged a pair of 4-ft.-wide doors, complete with original thumb-latch hardware, for his entry and reused a long, arched window from a demolished armory for the wall over his workbench. He clad the building in board-and-batten pine, which has mellowed in the weather to a dull gray. "This building that we put up is well over a hundred years old," Martin says, "and it's going to be standing for another hundred at least."

To protect it from intense thunderstorms that roll through the area in the summer, Martin installed a system of lightning rods on the standing-seam metal roof. When the shop was finished it became home for Martin and his family while they built a house and a number of other outbuildings. Like the house, Martin's shop is heated with wood.

Furniture and Custom Canoes

Martin builds furniture in Early American, Mission, and Shaker styles, and also works as a carpenter and timber framer. But he'd rather be making strip canoes.

Martin makes canoes to traditional as well as to his own designs, mostly for clients who want custom touches. Short decks at stem and stern are what Martin calls "signature pieces," made from cherry, maple, and walnut. He also shapes canoe paddles to meet the specific requirements of his clients.

When he started, Martin made canoes from Western red cedar that had been harvested in British Columbia on Canada's Pacific coast. But Martin was bothered by the long-haul delivery, which seemed unnecessarily wasteful, and he objected to timber-harvesting practices in the Northwest. His concerns convinced him to switch to locally harvested white cedar. The ash used in canoe gunnels is also cut locally.

A Comfortable Shop and Lifestyle

After a dozen years of woodworking, Martin's shop is well outfitted. He splurged on a new cabinet saw, but he also has found and refurbished a good collection of used equipment. He scavenges antique stores for useful tools and has built a collection of mallets, drawknives, and planes. Some tools were inherited from his grandfather.

STATION MOLDS make a reusable plywood form for "The Leaf," a solo canoe that Martin designed. Strips of cedar whose edges have been milled into a bead-and-cove pattern are laid over the molds to form the hull and then finished with epoxy.

MARTIN POSTED THIS, his most important shop rule, on a chalkboard for the benefit of a 14-year-old apprentice. With local schools phasing out shop programs, young people interested in working with their hands have fewer options. Martin occasionally takes one in, offering instruction on making canoes or cabinets.

NEARBY LOUISE LAKE is a convenient proving ground for Martin's canoes, and it gives customers a chance for a test drive. Martin uses the lake well into the winter, for as long as it remains free of ice.

He even has managed to hold on to the Mattel Power Shop his parents gave him when he was 12, a tool that combines a drill press, disk sander, lathe, and jigsaw. "They don't build toys like they used to," he says.

There is more to it than a shop and a collection of tools. Martin has redirected his life, finding a deep satisfaction in the woods and hills around him. "It is profoundly quiet here," he says. His shop is 100 ft. from his back door, a short "saunter" past flower and vegetable gardens and a chicken house. And at the end of his road is Louise Lake where Martin test paddles every canoe he makes.